Ghantasala

Epitome of Tradition and the Individual Talent

Dr. Ranganath Nandyal

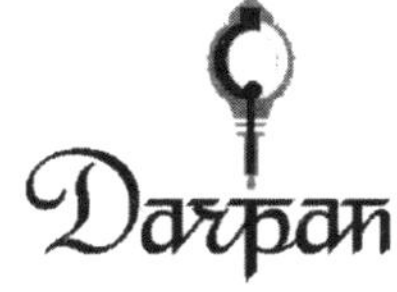

An Imprint of Prism Books Pvt. Ltd

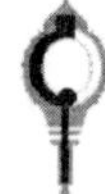

Ghantasala

Epitome of Tradition and the Individual Talent

Published by

Darpan – An Imprint of Prism Books Pvt. Ltd.

1865, 32nd Cross, 10th Main, BSK II Stage, Bengaluru -560 070

Phone: 080-26714108, Telefax : 080-26713979

e-mail : info@prismbooks.com | Website: www.prismbooks.com

Also at:

Chennai : 044-24311244, prismchennai@prismbooks.com
Hyderabad : 040-27612938, prismhyderabad@prismbooks.com
Kochi : 0484-4000945, prismkochi@prismbooks.com
Kolkata : 033-24297957, prismkolkata@prismbooks.com

e-mail: r.n.nandyal@gmail.com

Layout design : enablePrint, Bengaluru
Cover design : Bharath Agalpady, Bengaluru
Pages : 144
ISBN : 978-81-7286-159-9
Price : ₹ 275, 20 $
Printed at : Sreeranga Printers Pvt. Ltd., Bengaluru

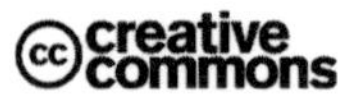

Dedicated to

My parents & My teachers &
Millions of Ghantasala's admirers

Author with eminent personalities

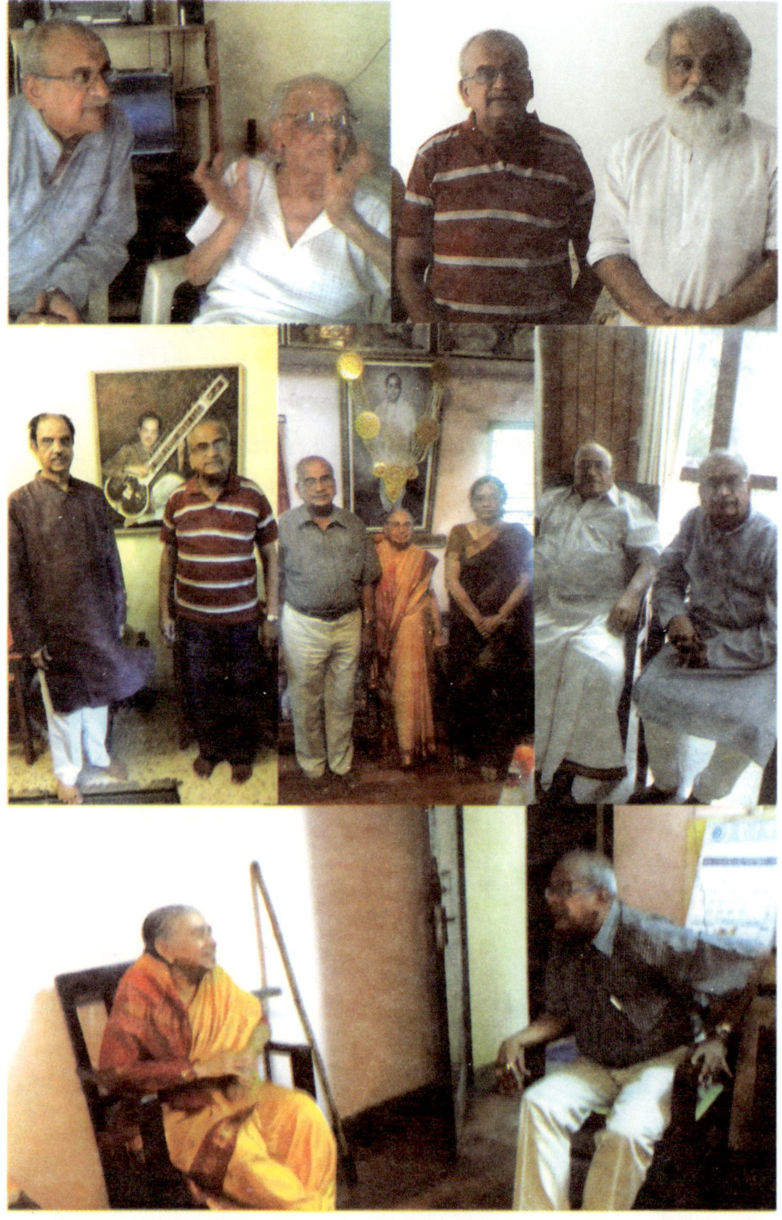

Preface

"Some are born great
Some achieve greatness
Some have greatness thrust upon them"
– Shakespeare

"Music is a piece of art, which creates an aural world of emotions"
– T. M. Krishna

"How deeply you touch another life is how rich your life is"
– Sadguru Vasudev of Isha Yoga Centre

Ghantasala was one of the versatile male playback singers of Indian cinema. Even today, 42 years after his sudden demise, if one hears his devout voice rendering a devotional song, an inspiring patriotic song, an exhilarating romantic song or a soul stirring sad song, one will have an upswing of emotions. No doubt that Sir S. Radhakrishnan told Ghantasala that he deserved international level recognition. As there is no book on Ghantasala in English till date, I thought I must write a book on the great singer-composer in English so that the students of Schools of Indian Music in abroad in particular and in India in general would be able to read it. Moreover, he deeply touched the lives of at least 4 generations of Indians: I proudly call myself an ardent admirer of the legendary singer-composer.

Mine is not a biography of Ghantasala. I have done research on Ghantasala as a singer as well as music composer. Having read the available books and articles on the subject of my research and having analyzed the internal as well as external evidence, I have come to the conclusion that Ghantasala had deep roots in Indian classical music-Carnatic as well as Hindustani-and possessed amazing individual talent. In my research I have explored the areas or aspects hitherto untouched by the other authors. My present work is my humble tribute to the immortal singer.

I am immensely grateful to the following persons:

Smt Savitramma Ghantasala, for giving me her blessings and the necessary inputs. Her book entitled 'Ghantasala Jnapakalu' gave me a lot of information; Dr. K. J. Yesudas for his touching tribute to Ghantasala. Shri Ratnakumar Ghantasala for his honest and humble Foreword; Shri S. P. Balasubramanyam for his hearty good wishes; Dr. K. V. Rao for giving encouragement at every step and a lot of material; Shri T. M. Krishna whose informative book: "A Southern Music: The Karnatic Story" helped me in shaping my book on Ghantasala; Shri S. V. Ramana Murthy and Dr. Sivarama Prasad for enlightening me on the classical ragas; Pandit Janardan for his valuable suggestions and support in Chennai; Dr. Rahmatullah and Shri Nukala Prabhakar for giving me the required information; Shri Venkateswarlu for his support in Bangalore and Shri Vamsee Rama Raju for his support in Hyderabad.

I cannot thank my wife, Padma Nandyal adequately for encouraging me at every step of my research on Ghantasala and for meticulously typing my manuscript. My special thanks to my daughter, Neeharika Nandyal for her suggestions and my son, Ved Nandyal for his love and affection. I profusely thank Shri S. Pranesh for getting the book published the way I wanted.

Tribute by
Dr. K. J. Yesudas

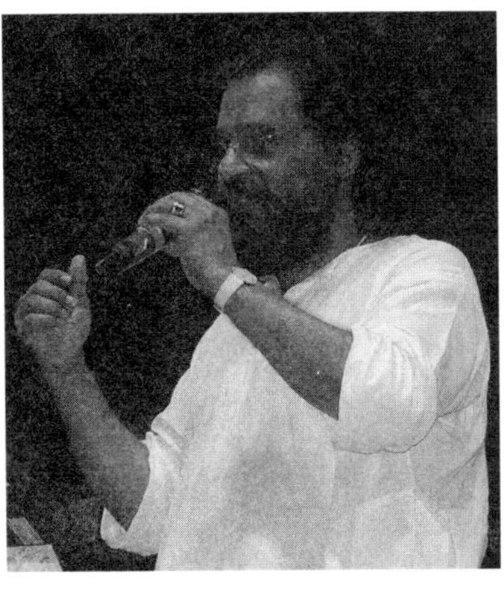

I offer my prayers to the Almighty God, the one and only creator of the entire Universe. If we think about anything, the entire creation is His creation. Now you can understand the impossible task for a human being to think about the total capacity and creation of God. We should think that everything is under the Almighty's control. Within that creation, there are some dedicated people that we feel and see. My father, mother and teachers played a great role in my life. Not only in my life, but parents and teachers play a very important role in everyone's life.

We all have been greatly influenced by many people in this small world, and especially by one of the greatest masters, Sri. Ghantasala garu. We music lovers can never forget him, his contribution, and the many generations that have been influenced by him.

In 1967, I was in Chennai, I could visit rehearsal camp near Boag Road. for a Telugu song composing by gantsala Garu for Smt. P. Leela, one of the great singers during our time. She took me to introduce the great man, who was none other than the great Sri. Ghantasala garu. One of the greatest occasions in my life was when I got to meet the legend.

Wish you all the best in your venture. And thanks to all the music lovers and fans of the Late Sri. Ghantasala garu.

S. P. Balasubramaniam's Good Wishes

Dear Sri Ranganath,
Compliments to you for writing the biography of Sri. Ghantasala in English.
I did it in Telugu (Mana Ghantasala) and wanted it to be translated into English. Some how, it did not happen and I was always uncomfortable about that.
Now you are giving solace to me by your work.
You are very right in getting it in English because, it will certainly enlighten the present generation who does not have the in depth knowledge of the genius, as most of them unfortunately cannot read and write Telugu and caught up in the whirlpool of the present day music (so called) only.
As many books come about the Maestro, yet there will be some thing left out about him.
I am eagerly awaiting to have your book.
Compliments and Congratulations to you
Balu..

Lata Mangeshkar's Tribute to Ghantasala

Lata Mangeshkar

101, PRABHU KUNJ
PEDDER ROAD,
MUMBAI - 400 026.

10th January, 2000

SHRI.GHANTASALA

I had high regard for Shri.Ghantasala Venkateswara Rao. He was renowned as one of the greatest singers of Telugu cinema. As a music director, of course, he created memorable music. He was a multi-faceted talent and he will always be remembered for his unparalleled contribution to music.

Lata Mangeshkar

LATA MANGESHKAR

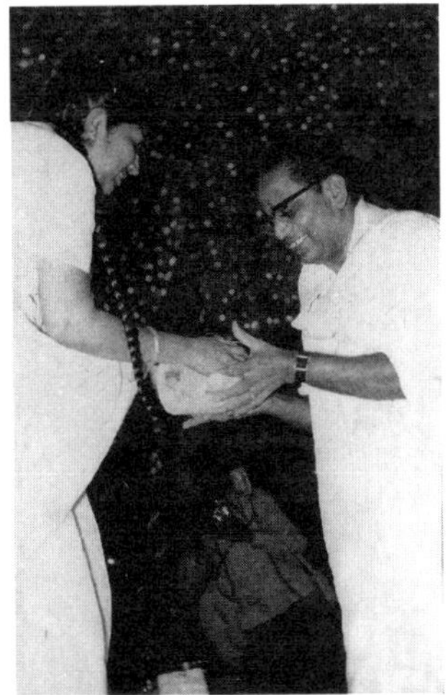

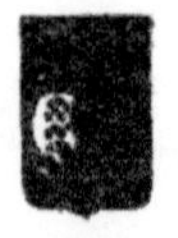

V. SHANTARAM

"SHANTSHREE"
Govt. Gate Rd.,
BOMBAY 12.

Aug 18, 1971

Dear Shri Ghantasala,

Though I never had any opportunity of seeing many South Indian films I have heard much about you as a proficient and consummate play-back singer. I was very happy to come face to face with you the other day when the South Indian Film Chamber of Commerce organised a function to felicitate me.

I am writing this brief note to convey to you my deep sense of gratitude for the love and affection you showered upon me on the occasion. I wish to say that I shall never forget the occasion or the sweet sentiments that you conveyed to me.

With my kindest personal regards,

Sincerely yours,

(V. SHANTARAM)

Shri Ghantasala Venkateswara Rao,
55, Usman Road,
MADRAS-17.

Contents

Foreword by G. Ratnakumar

"Shishurvetti Pashurvetti Vetti Gana Rasam Phanih"
(Music enthralls even children, animals and serpents)
–Traditional Saying

Several books have come on the life and times of my father, Ghantasala. Those were written from different perspectives. Every member of my family was elated to hear that a book on my father was coming out in English. My father was an embodiment of soul music and a personification of humility and politeness. The author of the new book, Professor Ranganath Nandyal has proved that Ghantasala's voice was God's gift to humanity and that he could sing beautifully at all the three Sthayees. The author has written extensively on the composing skills of the legendary singer and on the Carnatic and Hindustani ragas on the basis of which the immortal singer sang more than 10,000 songs. As Professor Ranganath has proved Ghantasala was indeed a pioneer in terms of singing melodious songs, sonorous Padyams, elevating Stotras and enthralling Kacheries of light music.

I hope and wish that this research work inspires many writers from different parts of the country to translate it into their respective languages.

Even though my father passed away in 1974, the very fact that a book is getting published in English in 2016 on the Legend, establishes his immortality.

Long Live Ghantasala!

G. Ratnakumar
Son of Shri Ghantasala
1st November 2016
Chennai

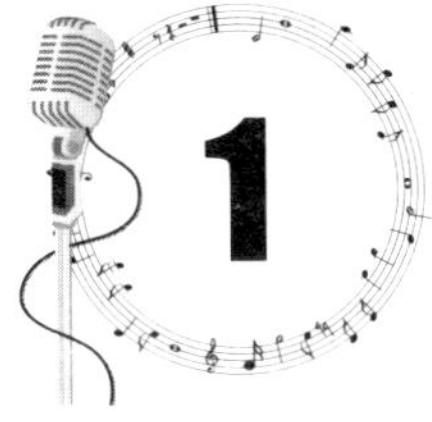

Formative period

The legendary singer Ghantasala Venkesteswara Rao was born on 4th December 1922 in a small village called Choutupalli, Krishna district (of Madras Presidency in British India which is in the present Andhra Pradesh). He was the third child of Shri. Surayya and Smt. Rattamma. Shri. Surayya played the Mridangam very well and sang *'Tarangalu'* and *'Ashta Padis'*[1] listening to which the toddler Ghantasala danced rhythmically. In this manner, the first guru for Ghantasala was his own father and his dances as a toddler got him the nickname, *'Bala Bharat'*. His musical voice got him fans amongst co-students, teachers and school inspectors. He studied up to the 9th class. When he was 11 years old, Ghantasala's father passed away which made him shift to his maternal uncle Ryali Pichchirama Shastri's house. In his last days Surayya told his son Ghantasala the greatness of music and asked him to attain *'Mukti'* (emancipation) by learning classical music from Vijayanagaram Maharaja College of Music. This advice of his father profoundly influenced Ghantasala.[2]

Neglecting formal education, he showed interest in Kapilavaayi Ramanathashastri's songs, *'padyams'* and played roles in Telugu plays like *'Chintamani'* and *'Sakkubai'*. In 1936, he went to Pedakallepalli for learning classical music from music director Susarla Dakshinamurthy's maternal grandfather Dattatreya Shastri. There, in spite of experiencing all the rigors of *'Gurukulavasa'*, Ghantasala's learning only managed to reach till *'Gitams'*. Being unhappy about the progress, Ghantasala moved to the place of a violin expert G. Nagabhushanam; there too his progress was not satisfactory. Having been vexed with the situation, Ghantasala decided to go to Vijayanagaram in accordance with the advice of his father. He sold off his gold ring and reached Vijayanagaram during the summer vacation of the Music College in 1936. [3]

Ghantasala met the Principal –Violin *'Vidwan'* Dwaram Venkataswami Naidu and expressed his desire to learn violin from him. Having listened to Ghantasala's sonorous voice, the violin exponent wanted the aspirant to pursue *'Sangeeta Sadhana'*. Had Dwaram not given Ghantasala the wise advice, remarked the playback singer, P. B. Srinivos, we would have listened to Ghantasala's violin performances instead of his melodious songs.[4]

Around the same time, as Patrayani Seetarama Shastry[5] moved from Saluru to Vijayanagaram Music College, providence turned a new leaf in the life of Ghantasala. Patrayani Seetarama Shastry was a maestro in **'carnatic'** music. From 1936 to 1942, Ghantasala focused all his energies on learning **'carnatic'** music and made best use of the able guidance given by Seetarama Shastry. At the farewell function organized by the Maruti Bhakti Mandali for the worthy.

'Shishya' (disciple) of a worthy *'Guru'* (teacher), Abhinava Kalidas Adibhatla Narayana Das presented Ghantasala with a *'Miraj Tanpura'*. Receiving a Tanpura and the blessings from the *'Apara Sangeeta Sahitya Saraswati'* [6] proved to be a good omen for the future of Ghantasala. [7]

The narrative on Ghantasala's apprenticeship period will not be complete without making a reference to the trials and tribulations experienced by the young music aspirant. When the 13–14 year lad wanted to learn classical music from Dattatreya Shastry, he had to go through all the rigors of a *'Gurukul'* and yet not go beyond *'Gitams'*. When the boy shifted to his relative G. Nagabhushanam's place, instead of enhancing his music skills, he was made to sharpen his culinary skills.[8] After selling off his gold ring, when the young aspirant reached Vijayanagaram, the vacation period for the famous music college had started. Can a 14 year old boy with ordinary qualities approach the principal of a college? Obviously, the boundless confidence and amazing determination present in the young lad – Ghantasala – made him approach the formidable Dwaram Venkataswamy Naidu for admission into the reputed college. Even though providence came to his rescue in the form of the advice given by the violin maestro and in the presence of the suitable teacher Patrayani Sitarama Shastri, the young aspirant did not have proper accommodation and food.

For the first two years, the young lad had to get his food by means of *'Madhukaram'* i.e. by using *'Angavastram'* like a sling bag, he had to go to a few houses asking for *food 'Bhavati Bhiksham Dehi'! Bhavan Bhiksham Dehi* [9] Whenever the boy did not get curry or pickle with *'Annam'* (cooked rice), he used to grind a green chilli in small pit and ate the food; the small pit used by the small – but budding – singer is preserved even today in the western staircase of the famous college[10].

Having seen the young lad's progress in learning music, Dwaram got him Maharaja's free mess facility. Even after getting back to his native place, Chautupalli, Ghantasala gave music lessons to girls of marriageable age [11] and played violin in the popular plays [12] for making both ends meet. The young graduate from Maharaja Music college, did *'Sangeet Kacheris'* during the celebrations like *'Sri Ramanavami'*, *'Saradanavarataris'*, *'Ganapati Navaratris'* and received the blessings of the maestros of the time like Hari Nagabhushanam, Parapalli Ramakrishnaiah Pantulu, Kroni Satyanarayana and Varanasi Brahmaiah Shastri.[13]

Being inspired by Gandhiji's clarion call for Quit India in 1942, the 20 year old Ghantasala joined the Indian National Congress party and sang inspirational songs in open air meetings which attracted the ire of the British and got him imprisonment for 18 months. When Ghantasala was in the prison, he had close encounters with stalwarts like Bezwada Gopal Reddy, Potti Sri Ramulu, Bulusu Sambamurti, and Erneni Subrahmanyam.

During this period, Ghantasala, with his sonorous songs, entertained the prison staff as well as his co-prisoners. He made use of his friendship with Moparru Das - an exponent of *'Harikatha'* - by learning *'Harikatha'* style of rendering. P. B. Srinivos in his book entitled 'Swaralahari'[14] says that Ghantasala used *'Harikathabani'* in rendering *'Sandhyasri Padyams'* like *'Anjanarekhavalganula'*.

Though Ghantasala had close encounters with the stalwart politicians of Andhra during his prison days, he left behind political life and got into *'Sangeet Sadhana'* again at Choutupalli. However, his native place did not give him steady earnings. When Ghantasala was in a state of sans employment sans money, his mother, Rattamma and elders in the family pressurized him to get married and so he did. His wife Savitri's native place is Pedapulivarru. Along with his wife Savitri, luck also entered Ghantasala's life. Providence turned a leaf in his favor.[15]

A Retrospective glance: From the stage of a toddler to the level of a young graduate from Vijayanagaram Music college, we have seen how Ghantasala passed through many a trial and tribulation and how he was fortunate to get an exposure to the stalwarts of the time – in music, literature and politics. In an interview given to Andhra Bhoomi[16] Sangita Rao – Ghantasala's assistant music director and son of Ghantasala's guru Patrayani Seetarama Shastry, testifies to the fact that quite often *'Sangeet Sahitya Sammelans'* took place in his father's home in which scholars, poets, musicians and novelists used to perform, discuss and make presentations on various aspects of music and literature. Those *'Sammelans'* are similar to the modern national/international conferences/seminars in which scholars from different parts of the country meet, discuss and make friends with the other scholars. It contributes to the growth of the budding scholars. In the same manner, the young music aspirant Ghantasala's exposure to *'Sammelans'* at his guru's place honed his musical as well as literary skills.

Ghantasala made use of both the sad as well as happy incidents in his life to his benefit. The sad incidents must have got into his subconscious and those memories intensified the sadness in his voice while singing sad songs like *"Jagame Maya", "Amma Nanna" and "Kanumusina Kanipinche"* and made the songs effective. His exposure to the maestros of music and literary giants made Ghantasala comprehend the connotations and denotations of words and their use while rendering the subtleties and complexities of a song. His natural devotion to the Divine power while facing problems, brought in the extraordinary *'Aarti'* in the rendering of *'Bhakti* 'songs[17]

Notes

1. Sri Narayana Tirtha wrote Sri Krishna Leela Tarangini: those devotional songs are called 'tarangalu' in Telugu. Ashtapadis are taken from 'Gita Govinda' of Sri Jayadeva
2. Ghantasala Savitri Ghantasala Jnapakalu Hyderabad: Sai Uday printers, 2012
3. P. B. Srinivos, Swaralahari: A Collection of essays on Eminent Music Directors Chennai: Kalatapasvi creations, 2014 *p*. 47
4. Ibid, *p*. 47
5. He was the father of Sangita Rao, an assistant music director to Ghantasala
6. Swaralahari, *p*. 47
7. Adibhatla Narayana Das was known as embodiment of literature and music.
8. Swaralahari, *p*. 47
9. In Sanskrit, it means 'Mother, give me food' and 'father, give me food'. The small pit is preserved even today.
10. A harikatha artiste Sarde Lakshminarasamma (Kalavaru ring) often gave the young aspirant some money whenever he felt the financial crunch.
11. In southern India, girls of marriageable age used to learn some basics in the classical music for singing before the prospective bridegroom/s and their relatives.
12. MeeGhantasala, GhantasalaAtma Katha, *p*. 29 Ghantasala, in those days, had an exposure to the stalwarts on the Andhra stage like Addanki Sri Ramamurthy, Parupalli Narasimha Murthy.
13. Mee Ghantasala, Ghantasala Atmakatha, *p*. 29
14. Swaralahari, *p*. 47
15. In Indian Astrology, if the 24 ganas out of 32 ganas match in the astrological charts of the bridegroom and the bride, the bridegroom would reach the top in his career.
16. Sangeeta Rao's interview given to 'Andhra Bhoomi' in Telugu
17. In a tribute paid to the famous singer V. Nagaiah, Ghantasala said: *"If a song has to be effective, the singer should have experienced the same 'rasanubhuti' (emotion) in his life"*.

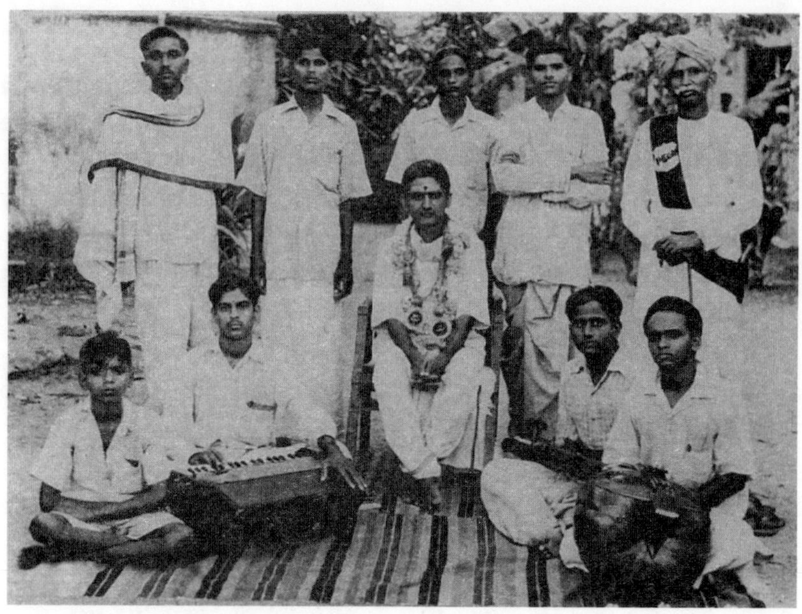

Mee Ghantasala, Ghantasala Atma Katha, *p.* 28 Nukala Chinna Satyanarayana, Nedunuri Krishnamurthy, Ayyagari Someshwara Rao, and Janagam Anjaneyyalu – who later became maestros in music – were still students by the time Ghantasala received 'Sangeet Vidwan' certificate from Maharaja Music College.

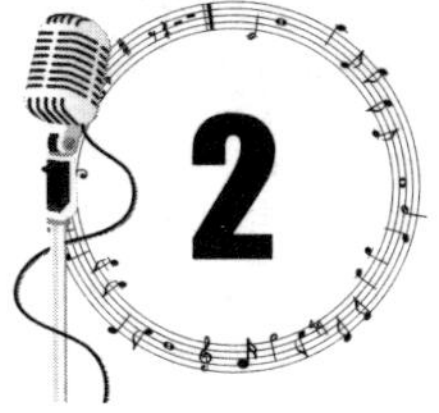

Pioneering Efforts

"There is a tide in the affairs of men, which taken at the flood, leads on to fortune"
— William Shakespeare

"Diligence is the mother of good fortune"
— Benjamin Disraeli

Nobody can predict the ways of providence. In '*Peddapulivarru*' village where Ghantasala married Savitramma, he met Samudrala Raghavacharyulu- who was by then well known in Madras film field. Senior Samudrala, having listened to the voice and observed the musical skills of Ghantasala, wanted him to come to Madras to look for opportunities.[1] Thus destiny led the young Ghantasala to Madras, the happening city and intellectual capital of those days. Having shifted to Madras in May 1944, the budding singer stayed for 3 months in the house of the well known lyricist. The magnanimous lyricist Samudrala introduced the budding singer to reckonable people in the film industry, got music concerts ('*kacheries*') done by him and guided him to meet the stalwart Rajinikanta Rao of All India Radio (AIR).[2]

The budding singer still faced some hurdles and obstacles: An officer in HMV rejected Ghantasala saying that his voice was metallic. Can you believe this? Later, Peketi Shivaram got into the position of the earlier officer and got the record done by Ghantasala in 1946.[3]

Tholeti Venkata Reddy was known to Ghantasala during his Vijayanagaram days. The patriot–singer's record containing

"Swaatanthrya me Maa JanmaHakku" (written by Tholeti) and *"Aa Moghul Ranadhiru"* (written by Prayaga) was released on 15th August 1947. Again in 1949 – after the demise of Sarojini Naidu – the patriot singer's another record containing *"Bharatiyula Kala Prabhavammolikinchi"* and "Amma Sarojini Devi" (both written by Tholeti) was released. Karunasri Jandhyala Papiah Sastry wrote "Pushpa Vilapam" in 1949. As Ghantasala was an adept singer-composer, he composed enticing music for the long poem and sang all the stanzas sonorously. The records came out in 1950.

In 1951, another record of Ghantasala containing *"Tenugu Bharati"* and *"Aasha Jeevi"* (both written by Tholeti) was released. Karunasri Jandhyala Papiah Sastry wrote "Kuntikumari" in 1951. Ghantasala deftly composed enthralling music for the long poem and sang all the stanzas mellifluously.[4] He further composed music and brought out records in 1955 containing the poems' Anjali", Karunamayi", Radhanura prabhu' and 'Regina mungurul.' All of them were written by Jandhyala Papiah Shastri.

Getting back to Ghantasala's career in the movies, he played small roles while contributing to chorus songs in G. Balarammayya's movie *"Seeta Rama Jananam"*. In Chittoor Nagaiah's *"Tyagaiah"*, he played a small role and sang a classical song for a role called Sundaresha Mudalliar. In B. N. Reddy's *"Swargaseema"* Ghantasala sang his first duet with Bhanumati, *"Oho Na Raja!"* In the movie *"Ratnamala"* of Bharani pictures, Ghantasala was given a chance to assist the music director Subburaman and to make tunes for some songs. In the movie "*Balaraju*", he assisted Galipenchala Narasimha Rao and composed most of the tunes; in the movie, Ghantasala sang his first song for Akkineni: 'Cheliya Kanarava'[5] Though *"Lakshmamma Katha"* was the first movie for which he composed music as its full-fledged music director, the movie *"Keelugurram"*- for which he composed music independently got released earlier than "*Lakshmamma Katha*. In 1949, he became a permanent employee of Vijaya Productions. *"Shavukaru"*, *"Patalabhairavi"*, *"Pellichesichudu"* and *"Chandraharam"* got him astounding success in series. Since then till his death in 1974, Ghantasala did not look back as a music director. Except 10–15 movies, all the 110 movies for which Ghantasala composed music, celebrated *'Shatadinotsav'* (100days), *'Rajatotsav'* (25 weeks) or some other Utsavs.[6]

Ghantasala as a Pioneer: A pioneer is, according to Advanced Learner's English Dictionary, the first or among the earliest to open up new vistas of thought, research or development. This could be in any field of enquiry or enterprise. So, a pioneer is one of the first few people to be involved in the new enterprise.[7]

What was the situation in the southern Indian film field when Ghantasala entered it? Chittoor Nagaiah and S. Rajeswara Rao sang for themselves. M. S. Rama Rao sang some duets with C. Krishnaveni and his other songs were mostly background songs ('Nepathya geet') S. Dakshinamurthy also sang a few solos and duets. Ogirala Ramachandra Rao and Banda Kanaka Lingeshwara Rao also contributed a few songs.[8]

In this situation, Ghantasala with his mesmerizing voice entered the field of playback singing. To paraphrase P. Susheela, the famous co-singer of Ghantasala who sang thousands of duets with him, Ghantasala's voice was God's gift to humanity. He brought a special status and recognition to light music.[9] To quote S. Janaki, another co-singer of Ghantasala "If you ring a big bell, the vibrations will be heard for long. In the same manner, the songs sung by Ghantasala will remain in our ears and hearts forever... he is inimitable. He is unique."[10] With his virtuosity and sensitivity, Ghantasala blended classical improvisations with folk music and the skill made him a class apart, above all others in the field. In due course of time, he created his own 'Bani' (style of singing) and established himself as pioneer in the art of singing songs. Singing 'padyams' based on classical ragas was peculiar to Telugu culture. In those times, Telugu stage and plays were profoundly influenced by Maharashtrian stage- music and the singing style of Bala Gandarva, Master Krishna Rao and Narayan Rao Vyas. Telugu stage actors like Raghuramayya, Suribabu, CSR Anjaneyulu and and even Kapilavayi Ramanatha Sastry followed Maharashtrian Style. The resultant was a crude and coarse, harsh and hoarse Telugu 'padyam'. After Ghantasala entered the scene, [11] he modified the singing of Telugu 'padyams' by limiting the lengh of classical raga and making it sound delicate and elegant, melodious and mellifluous His sweet, melodious and resonant voice suited and made their rendition pleasing to the ears of a variety of listeners. To paraphrase the film critic VAK. RangaRao, Ghantasala made the tunes for the 'padyams in the movie'Tenali Ramakrishna' and his 'Bani' continued.[12] As Ghantasala's voice contains, expresses and induces devotion, his rendition of the'stotras' also became popular. Thus Ghantasala pioneering efforts bore attractive and appealing fruit with regard to singing songs and rendering 'padyams' and 'stotras'. To paraphrase Sangeeta Rao, a musician and the singer-composer's assistant for two decades whoever sings songs today and whoever renders 'padyam' or 'stotram', he invariably follows Ghantasala's 'Bani'(style of singing).[13] Moreover, till the advent of Ghantasala in the film field, there used to be kacheries of classical music. The singer-composer started a new genre called Kacheries of Light Music and he performed many kacheries.

In a TV interview, the famous music director, Pendyala said that Ghantasala was the only singer at an All India level – who could sing melodiously at all *'Sthayees' (levels) - 'Mandrasthayi' 'Madhyamasthayi' and 'Tarasthayi'*.[14] Patrayani Sangeet Rao expressed the same opinion in his interview given to *'Andhra Bhoomi*.'[15] P. Susheela was also of the same opinion.[16]

"The science of music must be learnt: the art should be presented aesthetically"

– Nedunuri Krishna murthy[17]

"Ghantasala can easily perform a three-hour concert in carnatic music; it is the fortune of film field that he entered it and shone like the Sun."

– Nedunuri Krishna Muthy[18]

"Ghantasala led a rich, meaningful and artistic life"

– VAK RangaRao[19]

Why the producers and directors were after Ghantasala, wondered some curious minds. The explanation given by a famous director is noteworthy: "At the end of a day of busy shooting, we do a review of the scenes in the preview theatre: sometimes a scene looks stale and lifeless; the reason could be the deficiency in the screenplay, inability of the actor or ineffectiveness of dialogues.

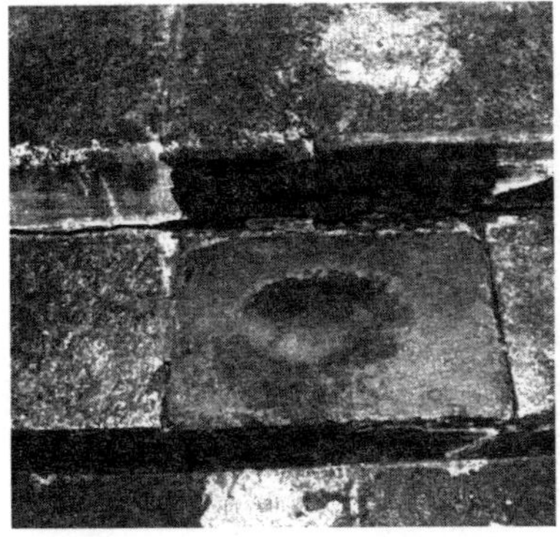

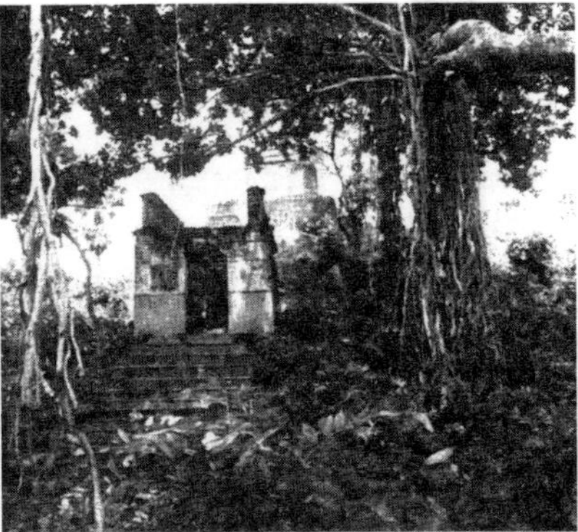

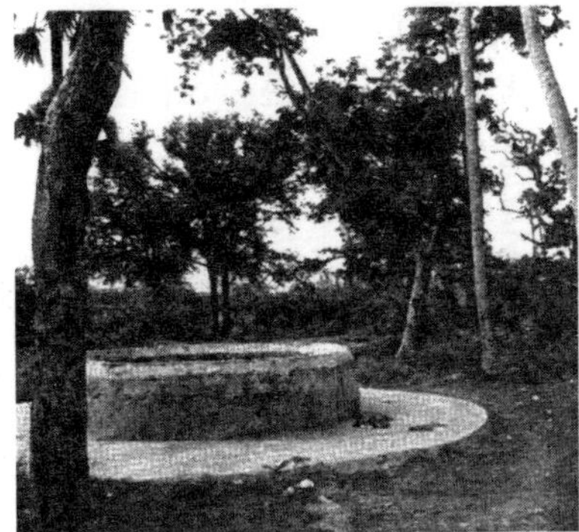

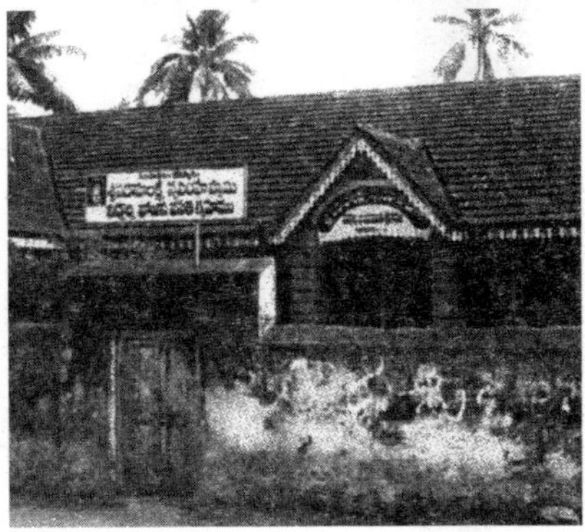

Then we remember Ghantasala as a rescuer: if we get a song written on the basis of the situation and make Ghantasala sing it, then the hitherto lifeless scene comes alive; when the audience listen to Ghantasala, they get mesmerized and forget about the scene." [20]

The mood of the song should get into him; he has to meditate on the song-keeping in view the idiolect of the actor i.e. the language features like intonation, tone and tenor and the situation in which it should be sung; then he says he is ready for a 'take' and is willing for any number of 'takes' for his satisfaction and the music composer's. This sagacious attitude made his songs distinct and brought permanence to his music.

Thus Ghantasala was bankable-both literally and metaphorically. He was dependable as he was willing to go for any number of 'takes' and his mesmerizing voice brought pots of money to the producers.

Some of the prominent songs sung by Ghantasala were based on the following ragas: [21]

Music Composer	Raaga	Song	Movie
C. R. Subburaman	Kalyani	*"Kudi Edamaithe"*	Devadas
C. R. Subburaman	Sindhubhairavi	*"Jagame Maaya"*	Devadas
C. R. Subburaman	Vakulabharanam	*"Kala Idani Nijamidani"*	Devadas
C. R. Subburaman	Pahadi	*"Cheliya Ledu Chelimi Ledu"*	Devadas
C. R. Subburaman	Yaman	*"O Devada.."*	Devadas
C. R. Subburaman	Sindhubhairavi	*"O Payanamaye Priyatama"*	Laila Majnu
C. R. Subburaman	Vakulabharanam	*"Ravo Nanu Marachitivo"*	Laila Majnu
C. R. Subburaman	Abheri	*"Andame Aanandam.."*	Bratuku Teruvu
Gali Penchala	Nata Bhairavi	*"Cheliya Kanarava"*	Balaraju
Gali Penchala	Sankarabharanam	*"Kanarara Kailasha Nivasa"*	Sita Rama Kalyanam
Gali Penchala	Kalyani	*" Sarasala Javaralanu"*	Sita Rama Kalyanam
S. Rajeshwara Rao	Kalyani	*"Kila Kila Navuulu Chilikina"*	Chaduvu Kunna Ammayyilu
S. Rajeswara Rao	Yaman Kalyan	*"Jagame Maarinadi"*	Desadrohulu

S. Rajeswara Rao	Bhimpalas	*"Yaramita Vanamalina"*	Bhakta Jayadeva
S. Rajeswara Rao	Hameer Kalyani	*"Nee Madhu Murali Gana"*	Bhakta Jayadeva
S. Rajeswara Rao	Jayjayvanti	*"Vadasi Yadi Kninchidapi"*	Bhakta Jayadeva
S. Rajeswara Rao	Mohana	*"Ratisukha Saare Gatimabhisaare.."*	Bhakta Jayadeva
S. Rajeswara Rao	Ragamalika	*"Pralaya Payodhi Jale"*	Bhakta Jayadeva
S. Rajeswara Rao	Yaman	*"Naduprema Bhagyarasi"*	Bhakta Jayadeva
S. Rajeswara Rao	Jayjayvanti	*"Manasuna Manasai"*	Dr. Chakravarti
S. Rajeswara Rao	Mohana+ Kalyani	*"Ee Mounam Ee Bidiyam"*	Dr. Chakravarti
S. Rajeswara Rao	Gauri Manohari	*"Nee Adugulona Aduguve"*	Poolarangadu
S. Rajeswara Rao	Sankarabharanam	*"Oka poola Bhanam"*	Atma Gourawam
S. Rajeswara Rao	Nata Bhairavi	*"Ranani Ralenani Oorake"*	Atma Gourawam
S. Rajeswara Rao	Kaafi	*"Kondalanni Vedikenu"*	Vasanta Sena
S. Rajeswara Rao	Madhyamavati	*"Jebu Lo Bomma"*	Raju Peda
S. Rajeswara Rao	Udayaravichandrika	*"Niluvuma Niluvuma Neela.."*	Amarasilpi Jakanna
S. Rajeswara Rao	Mohana	*"Ee Nallani Raalalo"*	Amarasilpi Jakanna

S. Rajeswara Rao	Kaanada	*"Madhura Maina jeevitala ..."*	Amarasilpi Jakanna
S. Rajeswara Rao	Mohana	*"Echatanundi Veecheno Ee ..."*	Appu Chesi Pappu Kudu
S. Rajeswara Rao	Madhyamavati	*"Kasi Ki Poyanu Ramahari"*	Appu Chesi Pappu Kudu
S. Rajeswara Rao	Mishra Hari Kambhogi	*"Sundaranglanu chuchi"*	Appu Chesi Pappu Kudu
S. Rajeswara Rao	Kaafi	*"O Panchavannela Chilaka"*	Appu Chesi Pappu Kudu
S. Rajeswara Rao	Abheri	*"Ninna Kanipinchindi"*	Rani Ratnaprabha
S. Rajeswara Rao	Pahadi	*"Muripinche Andale"*	Bobbili Yuddham
S. Rajeswara Rao	Sankarabharanam+ Khamboji	*"Andala Ranive Nevanta"*	Bobbili Yuddham
S. Rajeswara Rao	Pahadi	*"Kush Kushi Ga Navuuthu"*	Iddaru Mitrulu
S. Rajeswara Rao	Yaman Kalyan+Kafi	*"Ee Musi Musi Navuula"*	Iddaru Mitrulu
S. Rajeswara Rao	Sankara(Hindusthani)	*"Hello Hello O Ammayyi"*	Iddaru Mitrulu
S. Rajeswara Rao	Pahadi	*"Ouna Nijamena"*	Malleshwari
S. Rajeswara Rao	Shudh Sarang	*"Parugulu Teeyali"*	Malleshwari
S. Rajeswara Rao	Abheri	*"Akashaveedhilo Hayiga"*	Malleshwari

S. Rajeswara Rao	Kalyani	*"Chelikadu Ninne Rammani"*	Kulagotralu
S. Rajeswara Rao	Shuddha Dhanyasi	*"Neeli kurula Vannela"*	Kulagotralu
S. Rajeswara Rao	Sankarabharanam	*"Joruga Husharuga"*	Bharya Bharthalu
S. Rajeswara Rao	Abheri	*"Madhuram Madhram Ee ..."*	Bharya Bharthalu
S. Rajeswara Rao	Natabhairava	*"O Sukumara Nanu Chera"*	Bharya Bharthalu
S. Rajeswara Rao	Abheri	*"Challa Ga Ravela"*	Bale Ramudu
S. Rajeswara Rao	Kharahara Priya	*"Paataku Pallavi Pranam"*	Sangeeta Lakshmi
S. Rajeswara Rao	Thodi	*"Gandhiputina Desamaidi*	Pavitra Bandham
S. Rajeswara Rao	Madhyamavati	*"Oho ho Mavayya Idi ..."*	Aaradhana
S. Rajeswara Rao	Sankarabharanam	*"Na Hridayamlo Needurinche"*	Aaradhana
S. Rajeswara Rao	Mohana+Bilahari	*"Karunalawala Idineeduleela"*	Chenchu Lakshmi
S. Rajeswara Rao	Rageshwari	*"Anandamaye Alineelaveni"*	Chenchu Lakshmi
S. Rajeswara Rao	Yaman	*"Kallalo Pellipandiri"*	Atmeeyulu
Master Venu	Misramadhyamavati	*"Idiye Haayi Kalupumu Cheyi"*	Rojulumarayi
Master Venu	Madhyamavati	*"Akaasa Veedhilo"*	Mangalyabalam

Master Venu	Peelu+Natabhairavi	*"Vaadinapule Vikasinachene"*	Mangalyabalam
Master Venu	Charukesi+ Mayamalavagowla	*"Vuredi Peredi O Chandamama"*	Rajamakutam
Master Venu	Charukesi	*"Eee Pagalu Reyiga Pandu …"*	Sirisampadalu
Master Venu	Madhyamavati	*"Nee Sukhame Ne Korukunna"*	Muralikrishna
Master Venu	Sankarabharanam	*"Eenati Reyi Jabbilli Hayi"*	Kumkumarekha
S. Dakshinamurthy	Sindhubhairavi	*"Samsaram Samsaram"*	Samsaram
S. Dakshinamurthy	Behag Rag	*"Nidurapora Tammuda"*	Santhanam
S. Dakshinamurthy	Shanmukhapriya	*"Devi Sridevi"*	Santhanam
S. Dakshinamurthy	Kalyani	*"Challani Vennelalo"*	Santhanam
S. Dakshinamurthy	Bauli	*"Kanumoosina Kanipenche"*	Santhanam
S. Dakshinamurthy	Nata	*"Jaya Gana Nayaka Vighna"*	Nartanasala
S. Dakshinamurthy	Dhanyasi	*"Adinadi Giriraja Suta"*	Nartanasala
S. Dakshinamurthy	Peelu	*"Evvari Kosam Ee Mandahasa"*	Nartanasala
S. Dakshinamurthy	Sankarabharanam	*"Vagaladi Vaiyyari"*	Annapoorna
Pendyala	Sindhubhairavi	*"Nadireyi E Jamulo"*	Rangula Raatnam

Pendyala	Sindhubhairavi	*"Inte Ra Ee Jeevatam"*	Rangula Raatnam
Pendyala	Vijayanandachandrika (Chakravaka+ Kanada)	*"Rasikaraja Taguvaramu"*	Jayabheri
Pendyala	Abheri	*"Raagamayi Raave"*	Jayabheri
Pendyala	Maand	*"Needana Nannadira ninne"*	Jayabheri
Pendyala	Sindubhairavi	*"Nanduni Charitamu Vinuma"*	Jayabheri
Pendyala	Kalyani	*"Madisaradadevi Mandirame"*	Jayabheri
Pendyala	Abheri	*"Neelimeghaalalo"*	Baavamaradallu
Pendyala	Kaafi	*"Payaniche Mana Valapula"*	Baavamaradallu
Pendyala	Behag	*"Hridayama O Bela Hridayama"*	Baavamaradallu
Pendyala	Ragamalika	*"Mukkoti Devatalu Okkatainaru"*	Baavamaradallu
Pendyala	Abheri	*"Padi Mandi Lo Paata Padina"*	Ananda Nilayam
Pendyala	Darbari Kanada	*"Shivashankari"*	Jagadekaveeruni Katha
Pendyala	Bhageshwari	*"Raara Kanaraara"*	Jagadekaveeruni Katha
Pendyala	Des	*"O Cheli Oho Saki"*	Jagadekaveeruni Katha
Pendyala	Mohana	*"Aina Demo Ainadi Priya"*	Jagadekaveeruni Katha

Pendyala	Kalyani	*"Haayi Haayi Ga"*	Velugu Needalu
Pendyala	Madhyamavati	*"O Rangayo Poola Rangayo"*	Velugu Needalu
Pendyala	Arabhi	*"Tapamu Phalichinina"*	Sri Krishnarjuna Yudham
Pendyala	Mohana	*"Manusu Parimalinchene"*	Sri Krishnarjuna Yudham
Pendyala	Sindubhairavi	*"Chalada ee Pooja Devi"*	Sri Krishnarjuna Yudham
Pendyala	Abheri	*"Chigurakulalo Chilakamma"*	Donga Ramudu
Pendyala	Kharahara priya	*"Cherasala Palainava"*	Donga Ramudu
Pendyala	Bhageshwari	*"Mantalu Repe Nelaraja"*	Ramu
Pendyala	Bhimpalas	*"O Nelaraja Vennela ..."*	Bhatti Vikramarka
Pendyala	Retigowla+AnandaBhairavi	*"Seshashaila Vaasa"*	Sri Venkateshwara Mahatmyam..
Pendyala	Bhimpalas	*"Kalaga Kammani Kalaga"*	Sri Venkateshwara Mahatmyam..
Pendyala	Sindhubhairavi	*"Evaro Tanevaro"*	Sri Venkateshwara Mahatmyam..
Pendyala	Darbari Kaanada	*"Hey Chandra Chuda Madananka"*	Satya Harishchandra

Pendyala	Khamas	*"O Cheli Kopama Anthalo"*	Sri Krishna Tulabharam
Pendyala	Bhilahari	*"O Ho Mohana Roopa"*	Sri Krishna Tulabharam
Pendyala	Mohana	*"Mohanaraga Mahaa"*	Mahamantri Timmarusu
Pendyala	Sindubhairavi	*"Idenandi Idenandi ….. "*	MLA
Pendyala	Aberi	*"Neevu Leka Nimishamaina"*	Bhagya Chakram
Pendyala	Aberi	*"Emito Ee Maya"*	U. C. G. Sankarula Katha
Pendyala	Kedara Gowla	*"Kalgantiva Cheli"*	U. C. G. Sankarula Katha
Pendyala	Bridhavana Saranga	*"Nee Leelalone Oka Hayile"*	U. C. G. Sankarula Katha
Pendyala	Aberi	*"Thelisindile Thelisindile"*	Ramudu Bheemudu
Pendyala	Kaanada	*"Srinagaja Tanayam"*	Vagdhanam
Pendyala	Madhyamavati	*"Vinnanule Priya "*	Bandhipotu Dongalu
Pendyala	Malayamaarutam	*"Kondagaali Tirigindi"*	Uyyala Jampaala
Pendyala	Mishra Sarangi	*"Idemi Lahiri Idemi Garadi"*	Eedu Jodu
Pendyala	Bilahari+Sankarab	*"Pade Pade Kannulive"*	Anuragam
Pendyala	Sama	*"Jayahe Nava Neela Meghashyama"*	Sri Krishna Vijayam

Adi Narayanarao	Malkaouns	*"Rajasekhara Nee Pai Moju Teeraledura"*	Anarkali
Adi Narayanarao	Bhairavi	*"Kalise Nelaraju Kaluvachelini"*	Anarkali
Adi Narayanarao	Ragamaalika	*"Haayi Haayi Ga Aamani"*	Suvarnasundari
Adi Narayanarao	Ragamaalika	*"Idiye jeevitanandamu"*	Swarnamanjari
Adi Narayanarao	Mohana	*"Ghana Ghana Sundara"*	Bhakta Tukaram
Ashwatthama	Misra Yaman	*"Kanulumataladunani"*	Mayanimamatalu
Ashwatthama	Sindubhairavi	*"Bhale Bhale Pavurama"*	Rechchukka
T. V. Raju	Hussaini	*"Raja Maharaja"*	Tingu Ranga
T. V. Raju	Mishratilang	*"Lokapriya He Shyamala"*	Tingu Ranga
T. V. Raju	Bhimpalas	*"Belavuga Kanajalavuga"*	Tingu Ranga
T. V. Raju	Bhimpalas	*"Ellavelalandu Nee Challani"*	Pichchipullaiah
T. V. Raju	Keeravaani based	*"Aalapinchana Anuragamuto"*	Pichchipullaiah
T. V. Raju	Arabhi+Sama	*"Jaya Jaya Sri Rama"*	Jaisimha
T. V. Raju	Mohana+Kalyani	*"Ee Nati Ee Haayi"*	Jaisimha

T. V. Raju	Mohana	*"Madiloni Madhura Bhavam"*	Jaisimha
T. V. Raju	Mohana	*"Ravela O Chandamama"*	Todudongalu
T. V. Raju	Ragamaalika	*"Hey Krishna Mukunda"*	Sri Paanduranga Mahatmy..
T. V. Raju	Natabhairavi	*"Neevani Nenani Tala"*	Sri Paanduranga Mahatmy..
T. V. Raju	Sindhubhairavi	*"Amma Ani Arachina"*	Sri Paanduranga Mahatmy...
T. V. Raju	Yaman based	*"Vannela Chinnela Dora"*	Sri Paanduranga Mahatmy...
T. V. Raju	Lalitha based	*"Hara Hara Hara Shambo"*	Sri Paanduranga Mahatmy...
T. V. Raju	Suddha Nayani	*"Ouna Kaada"*	Rechukka Pagatichukka
T. V. Raju	Sindhubhairavi	*"Kanulevela Chilipiga"*	Mangamma Sapatham
T. V. Raju	Rageshwari	*" Priyurala siggelane"*	Sri Krishna Padaveeyam
T. V. Raju	Kalyani	*"Adenanenti"*	Saptaswaralu
T. V. Raju	Kalyani	*" Rendu Chandamama"*	Bhama Vijayam

M. S. Vishwanathan&Ramamurth	Sindubhairavi	*"Chesedi Yemito"*	Tenali Ramakrishna
M. S. Vishwanathan& Rammurthy	Kambhoji	*"Gandu Pilli Menu Marachi"*	Tenali Ramakrishna
M. S. Vishwanathan& Rammurthy	Abheri	*"Evaru Neevu Nee Roopamedi"*	Premalu Pellillu
T. Chalapati rao	Darbari Kaanada	*"Veluguneedala Baatara"*	Parivartana
T. Chalapati rao	Kaafi based	*"Niluvave Vaalu Kanula ..."*	Illarikam
T. Chalapati rao	Yaman	*"Nedu Sreevariki …"*	Illarikam
T. Chalapati rao	Yaman	*"Evari O Nee Vevari O"*	Punarjanma
T. Chalapati rao	Kalyani	*"Vinnavinchukona Chinna Ko"*	Bangaru Gajulu
T. Chalapati rao	Sankabharanam	*"Oorantha Ankuntunaaru"*	Raithu Kutumbham
T. Chalapati rao	Anandabhairavi	*"Kasturi Ranga Ranga"*	Zamindaar
T. Chalapati rao	Madhyamavati	*"Mabbulo Yemundi"*	Lakshadikari
K. V. Mahadevan	Bhimpalas	*"Shilala pai Shilpalu"*	Manchimanasulu
K. V. Mahadevan	Hindolam based	*"Nannuvadali Neevu Po Levu"*	Manchimanasulu
K. V. Mahadevan	Ragamalika	*"Aho Andhra Bhoja"*	Manchimanasulu

K. V. Mahadevan	Madhyamavati	*"Mama Mama Mama"*	Manchimanasulu
K. V. Mahadevan	Pahadi	*"Ramayya Tandri"*	Sampoorna Ramayanam
K. V. Mahadevan	Mohana	*"Nanupalimpaga Nadachi…."*	Buddimantudu
K. V. Mahadevan	Pahadi	*"Paaduta Tiyaga Challaga"*	Moogamanasulu
K. V. Mahadevan	Pahadi	*"Eenaati Eebandha Me Naati"*	Moogamanasulu
K. V. Mahadevan	Sindhubhairavi	*"Muddabanti Poovulo"*	Moogamanasulu
K. V. Mahadevan	Madhyamavati	*"Gauramma Nee Mogudevar.."*	Moogamanasulu
K. V. Mahadevan	Kharaharapriya	*"Na Pata Nee Nota"*	Moogamanasulu
K. V. Mahadevan	Yaman	*"Totalo Na Raju"*	Ekaveera
K. V. Mahadevan	Hari Kambhoji based	*"Prati Raatri Vasantaraatri"*	Ekaveera
K. V. Mahadevan	Chakravakam	*"Cheekatilo Kaaru Cheekatilo"*	Manushulu Maarali
K. V. Mahadevan	Nata Bhairavi	*"Adagaka Ichchina"*	Dagudumuthalu
K. V. Mahadevan	Shankarabharanam	*"Gorinka Gutike Cher"*	Dagudumuthalu
K. V. Mahadevan	Shankarabharanam	*"Dhaname Ra Annitiki."*	Lakshmi Nivasam
K. V. Mahadevan	Shahana	*"Chuchi Valachi Chen."*	Veerabhimanyu
K. V. Mahadevan	Behaag	*"Rambha Urvasi Tala."*	Veerabhimanyu

K. V. Mahadevan	Mohana	*"Adigo Navalokam"*	Veerabhimanyu
K. V. Mahadevan	Shivaranjani	*"Anaganaga Oka Raju"*	Atmabandhuvu
R. Sudarshan & R Govardhan	Raagamalika	*"Deva Deva Dhavacha"*	Bhukailas
R. Sudarshan & R Govardhan	Raagamalika	*"Ramuni Avataram"*	Bhukailas
R. Sudarshan & R G.	Tillang	*"Neela Kandhara Deva"*	Bhukailas
R. Sudarshan & R G	Bhageshwari	*"Mantalu Repe Nelaraja"*	Ramu
R. Sudarshan & R Govardhan	Abhogi	*"Eevela Nalo Enduko"*	Mooganomu
R. Sudarshan & R Govardhan	Sankarabharam	*"Chinnari Ponnari Poovu"*	Nadi Adajanme
S. P. Kodandapaani	Kalyani	*"Toli Valape Pade Pad."*	Devata
S. P. Kodandapaani	Sindhu bhairavi	*"Alayana Velasina"*	Devata
S. P. Kodandapaani	Kalyani	*"Tholi Valape Pade Pa."*	Devata
S. P. Kodandapaani	Keeravani	*"Madhava Madhava O"*	Sri Rama Katha
S. P. Kodandapaani	Mohana	*"Ennallo Vechina .."*	Manchi Mitrulu
Joseph & Vijaya Krishnamurthy	Abheri	*"Nannu Dochukunduvate"*	Gulebakavali Katha

Joseph & Vijaya Krishnamurthy	Sankarabharanam	*"Ontari Nai Poyanu"*	Gulebakavali Katha
Pamarthi V. R	Yaman	*"Puvai Virisina Punn…"*	Sri Tirupatamma Katha
J. V. Raghavulu	Abheri	*"Ee Jevanatarangalalo.."*	Jevanatarangalu
J. V. Raghavulu	Sankarabharanam	*"Ee Andaniki Bandham"*	Jevanatarangalu

Some of the prominent Padyams rendered by Ghantasala were based on the following ragas:

Music Composer	Raaga	Song	Movie
S. Rajeswara Rao	Mohana	*"Nava Kala Samiti lo"*	Appu Chesi Pappu Kudu
S. Rajeswara Rao	Abheri	*"Guttu Ga Letha Remmala"*	Chaduvu Kunna Ammayyilu
S. Rajeswara Rao	Kalyani	*"Meghai Medura "*	Bhakta Jeyadeva
S. Rajeswara Rao	Kalyani	*"Yadi Hari Smarane "*	Bhakta Jeyadeva
S. Dakshna Murthy	Hindolam	*"Adi Thappani Maa Yamma"*	Nartanasala
S. Dakshna Murthy	Kalyani	*"Evvani Vakita "*	Nartanasala
S. Dakshna Murthy	Shanmukapriya	*"Anthati Rajachandrudu"*	Harishchandra
S. Dakshna Murthy	Simhendra Madhyama	*"Dalame Payyada"*	Harishchandra

S. Dakshna Murthy	Neelambari	*"Chaturambodhi Pareeta"*	Harishchandra
S. Dakshna Murthy	Mukhari	*"Koduka Yenni"*	Harishchandra
S. Dakshna Murthy	Darbari	*"Arayan Vamshamu"*	Harishchandra
S. Dakshna Murthy	Kaafi	*"Deva Brahmana"*	Harishchandra
S. Dakshna Murthy	Kedara Gowla	*"Javadata Erunga"*	Harishchandra
S. Dakshna Murthy	Madhyamavati	*"Kabolu Idi"*	Harishchandra
S. Dakshna Murthy	Mayamalavagowla	*"Mayameya Jagamme"*	Harishchandra
Pendyala	Bilahari	*"Telugadelanna Deshammu"*	Maha Mantri Thimmarusu
Pendyala	Kalyani	*"Sri Vidya Pura Vajra"*	Maha Mantri Thimmarusu
Pendyala	Darbari	*"Ennadu Vedarani"*	Sri Krishna Tulabharam
Pendyala	Kedaragowla	*"Emi Tapammonurchitino"*	Sri Krishna Tulabharam
Pendyala	Maand	*"Kasthurika Thilakam"*	Sri Krishna Tulabharam
Pendyala	Abheri	*"Mettina Dinamani Satyayu"*	Sri Krishna Tulabharam
Pendyala	Bilahari	*"Sakala Dharmanu"*	Jagadeka Veeruni Katha
Pendyala	Kalyani	*"Prana Samanalai"*	Jagadeka Veeruni Katha

Pendyala	Surati	*"Pavanam Baaye"*	Sri Venkateshwara Mahatya
Pendyala	Kamas	*"Chelipichastala"*	Sri Venkateshwara Mahatya
Pendyala	Madhyamavati	*"Ontivaada Nenu"*	Sri Venkateshwara Mahatya
Pendyala	Gowd Sarang	*"Yevaro Athadevaro"*	Sri Venkateshwara Mahatya
Pendyala	Abheri	*"Nanu Bhavadeeya"*	Sri Krishnarjuna Yuddham
Pendyala	Hindolam	*"Vasudeva Sutam"*	Sri Krishnarjuna Yuddham
Pendyala	Bilahari	*"Bhaliraa"*	Sri Krishnarjuna Yuddham
Pendyala	Madhyamavati	*"Thanunde Hari"*	Sri Krishnarjuna Yuddham
Pendyala	Mohana	*"Upakarambulu"*	Sri Krishnarjuna Yuddham
Pendyala	Kaafi	*"Aapadalu"*	Sri Krishnarjuna Yuddham
Pendyala	Mohana	*"Yeggu Siggulu"*	Sri Krishnarjuna Yuddham
Pendyala	Kalyani	*"Nallapilli"*	Sri Krishnarjuna Yuddham
Pendyala	Yaman	*"Adduvacchunatanchu"*	Sri Krishnarjuna Yudham
Pendyala	Bilahari	*"Okaninti Nevaru"*	Sri Krishnarjuna Yuddham
Pendyala	Bilahari	*"Pathulane Manchi"*	Sri Krishnarjuna Yuddham

Pendyala	Madhyamavati	*"Rushulu Munulunu"*	Sri Krishnarjuna Yuddham
Pendyala	Simhendra Madhyamam	*"Vachanaalu"*	Sri Krishnarjuna Yuddham
Pendyala	Madhyamavati	*"Dharani GarbhamuDooru.."*	Sri Krishnarjuna Yuddham
Pendyala	Madhyamavati	*"Anda Pinda Samhitulanell."*	Sri Krishnarjuna Yuddham
Pendyala	Kalyani	*"Pranaya Saugandhikam"*	Prameelarjuna Yuddam
Galipenchala	Raagamalika	*"Daanava Kula Vairi"*	Sita Rama Kalyanam
Galipenchala	Arabhi	*"He Parvatinada Kailasa"*	Sita Rama Kalyanam
Galipenchala	Atana	*"Nee.... Ituvanti"*	Sita Rama Kalyanam
Galipenchala	Sankarabharanam	*"Janakendu........"*	Sita Rama Kalyanam
Vishwanathan & Ramamurthy	Hindolam	*"Sutamatiaina Andhrakavi"*	Tenali Ramakrishna
Vishwanathan & Ramamurthy	Sriraagam	*"Meka Tokaku Meka Toka"*	Tenali Ramakrishna
Vishwanathan & Ramamurthy	Abheri	*"Ranjana Chedi"*	Tenali Ramakrishna

Vishwanathan & R	Simhendra Madhyama	*"Kalanan……."*	Tenali Ramakrishna
Vishwanathan &R	Kaafi	*"Ganjayi Taagi"*	Tenali Ramakrishna
T. V. Raju	Mohana	*"Vasudhalo Evaraina Bhadrali"*	Sri Krishnanjaneya Yudham
T. V. Raju	Abheri	*"Japamemi Cheseno"*	Bhimanjaneya Yuddham
T. V. Raju	Bilahari + Mohana	*"Ksheerabdhi pai Delu"*	Ummadi Kutumbham
T. V. Raju	Simhendra Madhyama	*"E Padaseema Kashi "*	Panduranga Mahatmyam
T. V. Raju	Arabhi	*"Srikaamini Kamithakara"*	Panduranga Mahatmyam
T. V. Raju	Kalyani	*"Munduga Vachchitivu"*	Sri Krishnavatharam
T. V. Raju	Kalyani	*"Okkani Chesi Nannichati"*	Sri Krishnavatharam
T. V. Raju	Mohana	*"Janda Pai Kapi Raju"*	Sri Krishnavatharam
T. V. Raju	Mohana	*"Santoshamuga Sandhi "*	Sri Krishnavatharam
T. V. Raju & A. R. Rao	Kalyani	*"Ardhangi Lakshmi"*	Chintamani
T. V. Raju & A. R. Rao	Kaafi	*"Kastabharitambu"*	Chintamani
T. V. Raju&A. R. Rao	Khamas based	*"Chuchina Vela"*	Chintamani
T. V. Raju & A. R. Rao	Sivaranjani based	*"Chadivithi "*	Chintamani

T. V. Raju & A. R. Rao	Shubha Pantuvaraali	*"Talliro"*	Chintamani
T. V. Raju & A. R. Rao	Bhairavi	*"Kaalindi"*	Chintamani
T. V. Raju & A. R. Rao	Thodi	*"Kasthuri Tilakam"*	Chintamani
R. Sudarshan	Hamsanandi	*"Chekonavayya Mamsamide"*	Kaalahasti Mahatmyam
R. Sudarshan	Kedaragowla	*"Chandahuthashu"*	Kaalahasti Mahatmyam
R. Sudarshan & R. Govardhan	Sriraagam	*"Swami Dhanudanaitini"*	Bhukailas
Pamarti	Kedaragoula	*"Savadheeshudu Pandava"*	Babhruvahana

The classical Ragas that constituted most of the songs in Southern film music[22]

Anandabhairavi	Chakravaka	Jonpuri	Malahari	Saranga	Todi
Andolika	Chandrakauns	Kambhoji	Malayamarutam	Sarasvati	Udayaravichandrika
Arabhi	Darbar	Kanada	Malhar	Sahana	Valaja
Abheri	Darbarikanada	Kaafi	Mohana	Sankara	Varali
Abhogi	Des(i)	Kalavati	Marwa	Sankarabharanam	Vasantakalyani
Amrtavarshini	Deshkar	Kalangada	Natabehag	Shanmukhapriya	Yaman Kalyan

Athana	Dhanyasi	Kalyani	Padadip	Simhendramadhyama	
Begada	Dharmavati	Kedaragaula	Pahadi	Sindhubhairavi	Revati
Behag	Durga	Karnatakadevagandhari	Pantuvarali	Sivaranjani	
Bhageshwari	Hamir Kalyani	Kiravani	Pilu	Sriranjani	
Bhairavi	Hamsanandi	Khamas	Punnagavarali	Subhapantuvarali	
Bheempalas	Hamsadhwani	Karaharapriya	Rageshri	Suddhadhanyasi	
Bhup	Hemavati	Kuntalavarali	Rageshwari	Suddhasaranga	
Bhupalam	Hindolam	Mand	Rasali	Suddhasaveri	
Bilahari	Jayantasri	Madhukauns	Ritigaula	Surati	
Brndavanasarangi	Jayjaywanti	Madhuvanti	Revati	Thillang	
Charukesi	Jhanjhuti	Madhyamavati	Sama	Tilakkamod	

Notes

1. Swaralahiri, *p.* 48
2. Ghantasala Jnapakalu, *p.* 23
3. Mee Ghantasala, *p.* 36
4. Ghantasala Jnapakalu, *P.* 36
5. Swaralahari, *p.* 50. 'Cheliya Kanarava' was first song by Ghantasala for Akkineni in the movie 'Bala Raju'. Akkineni – Ghantasala combination started then and went on triumphantly for decades.
6. Swaralahari, *p.* 51
7. Advanced Learner's Dictionary, 4th Edition, 2003
8. In response to my questions, the famous critic, VAK Ranga Rao gave me this information
9. Mee Ghantasala, *p.* 51
10. Ibid, *p.* 54
11. Ibid, *p.* 53
12. In an interview held about 3 years ago, the famous critic, VAK Ranga Rao gave me this information
13. Ibid, *p* 83
14. In a TV interview, Pendyala proclaimed this
15. In an interview given to 'Andhra Bhoomi', Sangeeta Rao said this
16. Mee Ghantasala, *p.* 51
17. Ibid, *p.* 117
18. Ibid, *p.* 117
19. In response to my questions, VAK Ranga Rao gave me this information about 3 months ago
20. Smrititarangalu, *p.* 47
21. For preparing this roster of ragas, I took a lot of help from S.V. Ramana Murthy, Principal Annamachary Music College and author of the book "LavaKusa" and Sivarama Prasad, author of 'E Ragamo, Idi E Ganamo'
22. Ibid

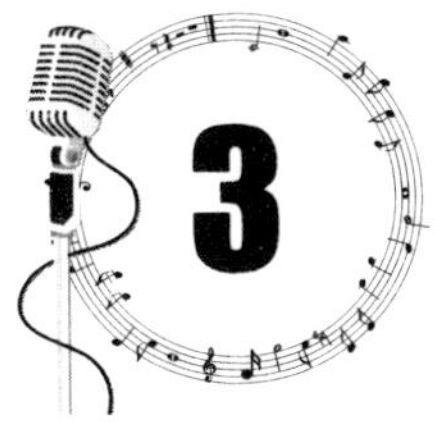

The Pinnacle: An Exponent of Indian Ragas

"Music is a piece of art which creates an aural world of emotions"

– T. M. Krishna, Musician and Musicologist [1]

"Art music is about creating art objects that are abstract creations, which give birth to an aesthetic form. The interaction between various components that constitute the music creates these artistic images. The result is an aesthetic experience without external intent".

– T. M. Krishna, Musician and Musicologist [2]

In rendering the songs based on classical ragas, Ghantasala followed the approach of his guru, Patrayani Sitarama Shastry. From his guru he learnt how to coordinate *'Sangeet'* with *'Sahitya'*. To paraphrase Ghantasala's words, while doing *'Gathrasadhana'*, one has to cultivate *'Shrutishuddi'*, *'Nadashuddi'*, *'Gamakashuddi'*, *'Taalagata'*, *'Swaragata'*, *'Layashuddi'* and in teaching all these techniques, his guru was an expert. Ghantasala assiduously cultivated the complexities taught by his guru and scrupulously followed them while composing or rendering cinema songs.[3]

Stalwarts like Pendyala, P. Susheela and Sangeeta Rao in one voice proclaimed that Ghantasala was the only singer at the national level who could sing melodiously at all the three *'Sthayees'*- i.e. *Mandra, Madhyama* and *Tara* 'sthayees.'

Dexterity of Ghantasala as music composer:

Realizing the potential of Ghantasala as a music composer, producer – actor C. Krishnaveni made him the music composer for three movies: *"Lakshmamma Katha", "Keelugurram"* and *"Mana Desam"*. Of them *"Keelugurram"* was first released and the songs of the movie became popular. In *"Mana Desam"* the multi talented composer used folk music in general and *'Burra Katha'* technique in particular, which received the acclaim of everyone.[7]

Having got the acumen to locate talent, the duo Nagi Reddy – Chatrapani took Ghantasala on the regular staff of Vijaya Productions. *"Shavukaaru", "Patala Bhairavi", "Pelli Chesi Chudu", and "Chandraharam"* got Ghantasala astounding success in a series. Nothing succeeds like success. Later *"Gunasundari Katha"*, *"Mayabazaar"* and *"Gundamma Katha"* of Vijaya's ten movies of Sundarlal Nehta's and scores of other movies of reputed directors and producers made him an enviable singer – composer in a vast country like India. He composed music for 110 movies in Telugu, Tamil and Kannada. To paraphrase a playback singer of the stature of P. B. Srinivos, all the movies; barring 10 to 15 for which Ghantasala composed music, celebrated Shatadinotsav (100 days), Rajatotsav (250 days) or some other Utsav[8]. Hemant Kumar, another singer – composer- who was a contempoary of Ghantasala- scored music for about 60 movies in Hindi and Bengali, but he was not as successful as Ghantasala in the fields of singing as well as music composing. Illayaraja – a successful music composer narrated an anecdote to the audience in a meeting in which Savitramma Ghantasala was present: when a producer asked Illayaraja to make every song of his movie a hit, the music composer retorted saying *"I am not Ghantasala to do such a feat"*.[9]

As a young lad Ghantasala was intelligent and diligent, receptive and sensitive, imaginative and creative. Providence led him to Vijayanagaram Music College where maestros like Dwaram Venkata Swamy Naidu and Patrayani Seetarama Sastry were available. In rendering the songs based on classical ragas, Ghantasala followed the approach of his guru, Patrayani Sitarama Shastry. From his, the sensitive and receptive young disciple learnt how to coordinate *'Sangeet'* with *'Sahitya' and why technicalities should not be pursued undermining 'Bhava' (mood or feeling).*

Being a diligent boy he did Sangeeta Sadhana everyday from 3 a.m. for hours together at Vyasa Narayana Temple located on a hillock near his college. Having practiced everyday, atleast for five years, Ghantasala got a command over the subtleties and complexities of ragas.[11]

His rigorous preparation must have lead to a level of internalization where the rules and grammar of the classical ragas and their aesthetics got embedded in his psyche. As the musician T. M. Krishna puts it: *"The spark of imagination leads to introspection and from the understanding that follows comes the creation."* And *"Every lived experience places a layer of impressions on our mind, and we build on it right through life."*[12]

In Ghantasala's life, every lived experience – pleasant or unpleasant – placed a layer of impressions on his mind. After he shifted to Madras in May 1944, the conducive atmosphere in the film world triggered the spark of imagination of Ghantasala, made him dwell deep into his psyche where his knowledge of classical ragas were embedded and the resultant was his creative output, nay, his mesmerizing music compositions in movies like *"Keelugurram"*, *"Manadesam"*, *"Shavukaru"*, *"Patala Bhairavi"*, *"Pelli Chesi Chudu"* *"Chandraharam"*, and in private songs like *"Pushpa Vilapam"* and *"Kunti Kumari"*.

In the crucible of Ghantasala's mind, his knowledge of carnatic ragas amalgamated with his exposure to folk music, *"Harrikathas"*, *"Burra Kathas"*, *"Bhavageet"* and his intimate knowledge of Hindusthani ragas which he acquired due to his close association with Bade Ghulam Ali Khan.

Moreover, the penance of practice – *"Tapasya"* – Ghantasala had done for years together equipped him to undertake improvisation. His focus was on the beauty of the language, its sounds- acoustic and emotive- syllables and their interactions with "raga" and "tala".[13] As playback singer, he had to focus on the situation and idiolect of the actor also. **(Idiolect is the variety of language unique to the individual)**

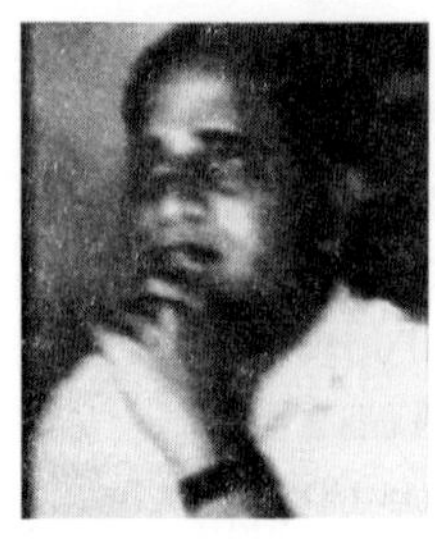

Ghantasala's imagination, *"transforming into creativity through introspection, understanding and improvisation"* was what imbued him *"with an identifiable and distinct creative personality"*. It reflected in all the movies composed by him. Among the audience, there would be all kinds of people: some could be cursory listeners, some discerning listeners, some with expertise in the field; among them the comprehending or cognitive abilities would be at different levels. Ghantasala's music and songs were appreciated by all categories of people. Even though maestros of music like S. Rajeswara Rao, S. Dakshinamurty, Pendyala, Adi Narayana Rao, T. V. Raju and Master Venu were his contemporaries, Ghantasala withstood the competition and succeeded in composing melodious music for 110 movies. Also, the singer- composer not only had a command over classical music but also embodied S. Rajeswara Rao creativity, Pendyala's smoothness and sweetness, Adi Narayana Rao's skill to utilize Hindusthani ragas and Master Venu's deft handling of the orchestra. In this regard he was comparable to Naushad Ali of Hindi film field whom he admired. Ghantasala deftly handled the orchestra from the beginning which reflected in the movies like *"Shavukaru" and "Pelli Chesi Chudu"* whereas S. Rajeswara Rao use of the orchestra could be seen more in his later movies than the former movies.[14]

"Improvisational music is what is referred to as Mano Dharma Sangeeta or the music that issues out of the individual musician's very own and personal musical sensibility. In other words, the music that is generated by the musician's distinctive imagination and creativity"[15]

–T. M. Krishna,
***Musician* and Musicologist**

"Ghantasala laid the foundation for the tradition of play back singing in films. His songs will permanently remain in the hearts of the people."
– M. Balamurali Krishna, Musician[16]

"When I have done music composing, for creating an effect I occasionally used a 'swara' which is not present in the raga and whenever I used the particular'swara,' I used it in the same symmetry and incidentally created another raga. I could have given another name to it, but I haven't given."

– Ghantasala[17]

As a music composer, Ghantasala's favorite ragas are: Kalyani, Bhimpalas, Rageshwari, Maund, Malkauns, Sindhubhairavi, Hamsaanandi and Hamsadwani. As a distinct creative personality – following his Manodharma – Ghantasala made some experiments. For example, in Kalyani raga, if the swaras are sung in this manner: dha, ni/ri/ga, ma, dha, pa, ma, ga, ri/ni...ga, ri, ga/ri, sa/; you can say that it is the patent of Ghantasala. [18]

Out of the 110 movies for which Ghantasala composed music, 80% of the songs were set to carnatic classical ragas. He was the music composer to compose film songs in ragas like chaarukesi, ahirbhiravi for the first time.[19]

a. *i.* *"Yevaro Yevaro"* in *"Pelli Chesi Chudu"* movie which was set to Chaarukesi

   ii *"Yedu Kondala Vaada"* in the same picture in Ahir Bhairavi

b. He used rare ragas like

i. **Soudaamini** (S G1 M2 P N2 S – S N2 P M2 G1 S) in *"Ooohalu Gusa Gusa"* from the film *"Bandipootu"*

ii. **Lathaantha Priya/ Guna Kriya** (S R1 M1 P D1 S – S D2 P M1 R1 S) in *"Toorpu Dhikkuna Adhigo"*... private padyam written by Arudra

iii. **Thillang** – *"Veliginchave Chinni Valapu Deepam"* private song and *"Naa Chandamama"* in *"Paandava Vanavaasam"*

c. He composed the following songs in *'raga Hindola'* by using *'Panchamam'* and *'Saadhaarana Gaandhaara'*; unlike how it is constructed (the raga doesn't have *'panchamam'* and uses *'Antara Gaandhara'* instead.)

d. *"Sandehinchaku Mamma"* – from the film "Lavakusa"

i. *"Karuna Choodavayya"* - from the film *"Deepavali"*
ii. "Sariyaaa Naatho" - from the film *"Deepavali"*
iii. *"Kalanaina Nee Valape"*- from the film *"Shanthi Niyaasam"*

e. Kalyani Raga was his favourite raga in which he composed several songs; also, he not only composed in Carnatic ragas but also in Hindustani ragas like

i. Sind*hubhairavi*
ii. *Bhimpalas*
iii. *Yaman Kalyan*
iv. *Gurjari Thodi*
v. *Bhupali*
vi. *Durga*
vii. *D*es

f. Several songs inspired by Bade Gulam Ali Khan especially in raga raageeshwari and Dwijaavanthi

g. In the movie "Rahasyam" Girija Kalyanam Yakshaganam was a unique composition as it has the following specialities:

h. He used 15 Janya Ragas in a singular composition as Janya Ragas are more than Ranjaka Ragas, those are:

i. Naa*ta*
ii. *Ataana*
iii. *Kambhoji*
iv. *Kedaragoula*
v. *Sahana*
vi. *Madhyamavati*
vii. *Saraswati*
viii. *Hindolam*
ix. *Reethigowla*
x. *Arabhi*
xi. *Vasantha*
xii. *Hamsaanandi*
xiii. *Saveri*
xiv. *Saama*
xv. *Ham*sadhwani

i. *Lalitha Bhaava Nilaya"* song from the movie *"Rahasyam"* was composed in the raga *'Saraswati'* for Goddess Saraswati; *'Sri'* Ragam for goddess Lakshmi and *'Lalita'* Ragam on Lalita Devi. This shows Ghantasala's keen observation. His experiment of using the raga corresponding to the relevant goddess was successful and marvelously tuned.

j. Another example of his prowess is:
'Vasantha Bhairavi' raga is a rare raga that Ghantasala composed a song in - *"Amba Jagadamba"* from the movie *"Shakuntala"* sung by P. Susheela and written by Sr. Samudrala. Nobody else but the great thespian 'Tyagaraja Swami' used this raga to compose *"Nee Daya Raada" 'kriti'*.

To cite some more examples:

i. The background music for the movie *"Keelugurram"*– created by using guitar, violin and piano- was not only enthralling but also contributed to the development of plot. [20]

ii. In *"Manadesam"*, the singer-composer skillfully made use of *'Harikathas'* and *"Burrakathas"* and made them an integral part of the plot.

iii. To paraphrase the words of well known music composer Ramesh Naidu: In today's film world, new techniques have come- especially in the sub fields of sound and screen play; new instruments – electronic instruments are being played; in recording procedures, modern mikes and mixers are being used; even though there are so many tracts today in recording, the sounds of anklets do not sound like anklets. In the movie *"Shavukaru"* Ghantasala created the real sounds of anklets; while *'Harikatha'* goes on, the song as well as dialogues are clearly heard; in "Deepavali Deepavali" song, crackers are clearly heard without disturbing the background song. Even though many facilities were not available in those days, Ghantasala and his team did focused work for bringing out quality product. [21]

iv. When the king – heroine's father and his family visit the Rajmahal of the hero, in *"Patala Bhairavi"*, the background music provided by the adept singer-composer was appropriate for the scene.

v. In *"Paropakaram"* the sounds of anklets and the music of the violin were enticing.

vi. In *"Sati Sukanya"*, the song *"Madhuramaina Reyi, Mari Raadu Ide Haayi"*, takes the listeners to another world and the instrumental music used contributed to the voyage to another world.

vii. In *"Mayabazar"* the special radar effect created, when Ghatotkacha (S. V. Ranga Rao) enters and sings a padyam, is incredible; similarly, during the song *"Daya Cheyandi Daya Cheyandi"* sung by Ghantasala and Madhavapeddi, the background music is memorable.

viii. In *"Pandava Vanavasam"* whenever the character Bheema (NT Rama Rao) enters and walks, special background music is played.

ix. The *prose ('Vachanam')* used by Ghantasala was not prosaic; it was poetic, musical and meaningful; it contributed to the sonoriety and flow of the song.

For example: -

*In the song *"Bhavi Bharata Bhagya Vidhathalara"* from the movie *"Pelli Chesi Chodu"*, the singer-composer's prose *"Vaarevva"* and *"Thadinna Thakadhinna Tangadi Tadhakita Tom"* and *"Tarampam"* enhanced the melody of the song.

*In the song *"Kolo Kolo Yamma"* from the movie *"Gundamma Katha"*, the adept composer's prose: *'Dik Dhinakdhina Dhik Dhinakdhina Dhik Dhinakdhina Dhik'* makes it bewitching to the listeners.

*At the beginning of the rendition of *"Pushpa Vilapam"* the prose used and the atmosphere created would tell the discerning listeners that Ghantasala was a genius.

*In *"Kunti Kumari"*, the singer- composer deftly used the prose as well as instruments like Hawaiian guitar as signpost

Some of the prominent songs sung by Ghantasala were based on the following ragas:[22]

Music Composer	Raaga	Song	Movie
Ghantasala	Hindola	*"Sandehinchakumamma"*	Lavakusa
Ghantasala	Mayamalavagoula	*"Enimishaniki Emijaruguno"*	Lavakusa
Ghantasala	Kaanada	*"Jagadhbhiraamudu Sriramude"*	Lavakusa
Ghantasala	Jhunjati	*"Veyyara Debba"*	Lavakusa
Ghantasala	Jhunjati	*"Vollanori Nee Pillani"*	Lavakusa
Ghantasala	Rageshwari	*"Rave Premalatha"*	Pillazamindaru
Ghantasala	Rageshwari	*"Annana Bhamini Emani"*	Sarangadhara
Ghantasala	Kharaharapriya	*"Chanduruni Minchu Andamolikinchu"*	Raktasambandham
Ghantasala	Kambhoji	*"Samsara Jaladhi Datinche Naava"*	Bhakta Raghunath
Ghantasala	Kamavardhani	*"Dinakara Shubhakara"*	Vinayakachaviti
Ghantasala	Brundavana Saran	*"Chupulu Kalasina Subhavela"*	Mayabazaar

Ghantasala	Mohana	*"Lahiri Lahiri Lahiri lo"*	Mayabazaar
Ghantasala	Abheri	*"Neevena Nanu Talachinadi"*	Mayabazaar
Ghantasala	Bhageshwari	*"Neekosame Ne Jeevinchunadi"*	Mayabazaar
Ghantasala	Jayajayawanti	*"Himagiri Sogasulu"*	Pandava Vanavasam
Ghantasala	Thillang	*"Naa Chandamama Neeve Bhama"*	Pandava Vanavasam
Ghantasala	Chakravakam	*"Vidhi Vanchitulai Vibhavam Kori"*	Pandava vanavasam
Ghantasala	Betag	*"Manasu Padindi Sannayi Paata"*	Punyavati
Ghantasala	Kalyani	*"Pelli Chesikoni Illu Chusukoni"*	Pelli Chesi Chudu
Ghantasala	Kalyani	*"Raave Naa Cheliya"*	Manchi Manasuku Manchi Rojulu
Ghantasala	Pahadi	*"Navvula Nadilo"*	Marmayogi
Ghantasala	Sindhubhairavi	*"Jayammu Nischayammura"*	Shabhas Ramudu
Ghantasala	Madhyamavati	*"Kalakalavirise Jagale"*	Shabhas Ramudu
Ghantasala	Abheri	*"Prema Yatralaku Brindavanam"*	Gundamma Katha

Ghantasala	Mohana	*"Veshamu Marchenu "*	Gundamma Katha
Ghantasala	Durga	*"Kolo Kolo Yamma"*	Gundamma Katha
Ghantasala	Madhyamavati	*"Lechindi Mahilalokam"*	Gundamma Katha
Ghantasala	Mohana	*"Maunamuga Nee manasu Padina"*	Gundamma Katha
Ghantasala	Abheri	*"Vennelalona Vedimelano"*	Pelli Naati Pramanalu
Ghantasala	Abheri	*"Kalavaramaaye Madilo"*	Patala Bhairavi
Ghantasala	Abheri	*"Pranaya Jeevulaku Devi Varale"*	Patala Bhairavi
Ghantasala	Rageshwari	*"Enta Ghatu Premayo"*	Patala Bhairavi
Ghantasala	Kalyani	*"Palukaradate Chiluka*	Shaavukaru
Ghantasala	Bhilawl	*"Emanene Chinari Emanene"*	Shaavukaru
Ghantasala	Kalyani	*"Saagenu Jeevita Naava"*	Thobuttuvulu
Ghantasala	Behaag	*"Manasu Paadindi Sannayi Paata"*	Punyavati
Ghantasala	Natabhairavi	*'Pedavula Paina Sangeetam'*	Punyavati

Ghantasala	Abheri	*"Enta Sogasuga Vunnavu"*	Punyavati
Ghantasala	Saudamini	*"Oohalu Gusagusalade"*	Bandi Potu
Ghantasala	Shivaranjani	*"Vagala Ranivi Neeve"*	Bandi Potu
Ghantasala	Bhageshwari	*"Madilo Maunamuga Kadile"*	Shakuntala
Ghantasala	Maund	*"Sarasana Nevunte Jabili"*	Shakuntala
Ghantasala	Sindhubhairavi	*"Kaadusuma Kala Kaadusuma"*	Keelugurram
Ghantasala	Sindhubhairavi	*"Shimhachalamu Maha Punya"*	Shimhachala Kshetra Mahima
Ghantasala	Rageshwari	*"Raagala Saragala"*	Shantinivasam
Ghantasala	Sankarabharanam	*"Come Come Come Kangaaru"*	Shantinivasam
Ghantasala	Rageshwari	*"Idi Na Cheli Idi Na Saki"*	Chandraharam
Ghantasala	Kharahapriya	*"Endaka Endaka Endaka"*	Chiranjeevulu
Ghantasala	Sindhubairavi	*"Kanupapa Karavaina"*	Chiranjeevulu
Ghantasala	Khamboji+ Sankarabharanam	*"Chikilinta Chiguru Sampangi Guburu"*	Chiranjeevulu
Ghantasala	Mohana	*"Tirumala Mandira Sundara"*	Menakodalu

Ghantasala	Natabhairavi	*"Neelo Nenai Naalo Neevai"*	Ali Baba 40 Dongalu
Ghantasala	Asaveri	*"O Ho Basti Dorasani"*	Abhimanam
Ghantasala	Kalyani	*"Nasari Neevani Neeguri Nenani"*	CID
Ghantasala	Abheri	*"Naaloni Ragameeve"*	Paramanandayya Shishula...
Ghantasala	Madhyamavathi	*"Malliyalara Malikarala"*	Nirdoshi
Ghantasala	Udaya Ravi Chandrika	*"Unnadi le Dagunnadile"*	Rahasyam
Ghantasala	Mohana	*"Tirumala Giri Vasa Divyamandahasa"*	Rahasyam
Ghantasala	Jalahari	*"Hridayama Sagipomma"*	Paropakaram
Ghantasala	Kalyani	*"Jabilli Shobha Neeve"*	Satyanarayana Maha..
Ghantasala	Ghaoorjari todi	*"Madhava Maunama"*	Satyanarayana Maha..
Ghantasala	Kuranji	*"Chilipi Krishnuni Toti Chesevu"*	Varasatvam
Ghantasala	Chakravakam	*"Gaali Veechenu"*	Chuttarikaalu
Ghantasala	Sindubhairavi	*"Jagadhirama Raghukulasoma"*	Ramalayam

Some of the prominent Padyams rendered by Ghantasala were based on the following ragas:

Music Composer	Raaga	Song	Movie
Ghantasala	Bhairavi	*"Jagadeka Ramabhayei"*	Vinayaka Chaviti
Ghantasala	Mohana	*"Pratah Kale Bhavet"*	Vinayaka Chaviti
Ghantasala	Asaaveera	*"Intaku Pooni Vacchi"*	Lava Kusa
Ghantasala	Begada	*"Ide Mana Ashrammamu"*	Lava Kusa
Ghantasala	Shankarabharanam	*"Navaratnojwala Kaanti"*	Lava Kusa
Ghantasala	Kalyani	*"Rangaru Bangaru Chengav"*	Lava Kusa
Ghantasala	Maund	*"E Mahaneeya Sadhvi"*	Lava Kusa
Ghantasala	Neelamani	*"Pratidena Menu Toldoluta"*	Lava Kusa
Ghantasala	Subhapanthuvarali	*"Achchate Kannuganaka"*	Paramanandayya Sishyulu
Ghantasala	Hindolam	*"Vande..........."*	Paramanandayya Sishyulu
Ghantasala	Mohana	*"Navanavojwala"*	Paramanandayya Sishyulu
Ghantasala	Kedaragowla	*'Manojavam maruta'*	Pandava vanavasam
Ghantasala	Jalahari	*"Hridayama saagipomma"*	Paropakaram

The rendition of the Bhagavad Gita slokas: the amalgamation of Carnatic and Hindustani Sampradayas

The Upanishads, the Brahmasutras and the Bhagavad Gita comprise the 'Prasthanatrayi' - the three pillars of the Vedanta. It inspired the great freedom fighters including Bal Gangadhar Tilak, Sri Aurobindo and Mahatma Gandhi. Modern sages like Swami Vivekananda, Sir S. Radhakrishnan, Swami Ranganathananda and Swami Chinmayananda interpreted the Gita for invigorating the people and for putting them on the right path to action. "Yogah Karmasu Kausalam" "Dexterity in action is Yoga," proclaimed the Lord of Kurukshetra. Being a Karma Yogi, Ghantasala realized the importance of the Gita in human life. As his wont, he kept in view the needs and limitations of the common man while selecting 108 Slokas out of 700 slokas[23]. Before Ghantasala sang the slokas sonorously, the Gita was only "Parayana Gita" in the houses of the Telugus; it has now become a habit for them to listen to Ghantasala's melodious rendition of the Gita. Ghantasala used his knowledge of the Carnatic and the Hindustani Samprdayas while rendering the slokas. For instance, in the use of the 'Pantuvarali'raga for the 'prarambha' sloka 'Parthaya Pratibhoditam' and "Surati'raga for the 'Phalashruti':" Gita Shastra Midam Punyam'the singer-composer's discretion amply comes out.[24]

To the common man it sounds as though Lord Krishna is teaching through the mesmerizing voice of Ghantasala. Some of the slokas rendered by the immortal singer are[25]:

S. no	Ragas	Chapter	Sloka. no	Sloka
1	Abheri	8	8	"Abhyasa Yoga Yuktena Chetasa....."
2	Abheri	8	9	"Kavim Purana Manu Shasitaram....."
3	Abhogi	8	21	"Avyktokshra Ityuktah Tama....."
4	Abhogi	8	26	"Shukla Krishne Gatti Hyeti....."
5	Amrutavarshina	3	3	"Lokosmin Dwividha Nishta......"

S. no	Ragas	Chapter	Sloka. no	Sloka
6	Amrutavarshina	3	14	"Annad Bhavanthi Bhutani......."
7	Amrutavarshina	3	16	"Evam Pravartitam Chakram......"
8	Aarabhi	2	72	"Esha Brahmi Stithah Partha..."
9	Eesha Manohari	1	32	"Na Kankshe Vijayam... "
10	Udaya Ravi Chandrika	9	26	" Patram Pushpam Phalam Thoyam.."
11	Udaya Ravi Chandrika	9	56	" Dhukhe Shanu Dwignamana..."
12	Udaya Ravi Chandrika	9	34	"Manyana Bhava Madbhaktho..."
13	Kalyani	16	3	"Tejah Kshama Dhruthi Ssaucham.."
14	Kalyani	16	4	"Dambho Darpobhi Manasha-------"
15	Kaafi	17	2	"Trividha Bhavati Shraddha ---"
16	Kaafi	17	4	"Yajante satvika devan------"
17	Kaafi	17	15	"Anudwaga karam vakyam---"
18	Kamavardhani			"Parthaya prati bodhitam----"
19	Keeravani	13	28	"Samam Sarveshu Bhuteshu---"
20	Kedaragowla	18	73	"Nashto mohah Smritir Labda---"
21	Khamas	4	39	"Sraddhavan Labhate Jnanam—"

S. no	Ragas	Chapter	Sloka. no	Sloka
22	Ghoorjari Todi	11	15	"Pashyamidevam Tava Deva----"
23	Ghoorjari Todi	11	16	"Aneka Baahudara Vaktra Netram..."
24	Ghoorjari Todi	11	25	"Damshtra Kalalini Cha Te...."
25	Chandrakous	11	5	"Pashyame Partha Rupani...."
26	Charukesi	5	2	"Sanyasah Karmayogascha Nih..."
27	Charukesi	5	10	"Brahmanyadha Karmani..."
28	Charukesi	5	16	"Jnanena Tu Tadajnanam...."
29	Jogiya	2	22	"Vataam Si Jeernani Yadha.."
30	Jogiya	2	23	"Nainam Chindanthi Chastrani..."
31	Jaulpuri	12	16	"Anapekshah Ssuchir Dakshah..."
32	Jaulpuri	12	18	"Samass Thraucha Mitrecha..."
33	Jaulpuri	12		"Tulyaninda Stutri Mauni..."
34	Tilaang	11	46	"Keeritanam Gadhinam Chakra..."
35	Tilaang	11	52	"Sudarshana Medam Rupam...."
36	Thodi	13	2	"Idam Shariram Kaunteya..."
37	Thodi	13	12	"Adhyatma Gnana Nityatvam..."
38	Thodi	13	21	"Karya Karana Kartrutve Hetuh..."

S. no	Ragas	Chapter	Sloka. no	Sloka
39	Darbhari Kaanada	2	11	"Ashochya Na Nva Shochastvam.."
40	Darbhari Kaanada	2	13	"Dehinosmin Yatha Dehe...."
41	Dhanyasi	14	8	"Tamastva Gnanajam Viddi..."
42	Dhanyasi	14	25	"Manava Maana Yostulyah..."
43	Des	4	19	"Yesya Survey Samarambha...."
44	Des	4	24	"Brahmarpanam Brahmahavihi..."
45	Peer	10	20	"Ahamatma Gudakesha..."
46	Peer	10	22	"Vedanaam Samavedosmi.."
47	Poorvi Kalyani	8	28	"Vedeshu YagneshuTapassu Chaiva.."
48	Poorvi Kalyani	9	7	"Sarvabhutani Kaunteya Prakritim.."
49	Poorvi Kalyani	9	22	"Ananya Chintayantomam..."
50	Bhilas Khan Thodi	2	27	"Jatasyahi Dhruvo Mruthuh..."
51	Madhuvanti	4	10	"Veetaraga Bhayakrodha......"
52	Madhuvanti	4	11	"Yeyatha Maam Prapadyante....."
53	Madhuvanti	14	1	"Param Bhuyah Pravakchyami...."
54	Malayamarutam	6	29	"Sarvabhutasta Matmanam....."
55	Malayamarutam	6	35	"Asamshayam Mahabaaho....."

S. no	Ragas	Chapter	Sloka. no	Sloka
56	Malayamarutam	6	47	"Yoginamapi Sarvesham......"
57	Mohana	4	7	"Yada Yada hi Dharmasya"
58	Mohana	4	8	"Paritrayana Sadhunam..."
59	Mohana	15	1	"Urdhva Moola Madha Shakam.."
60	Mohana	15	6	"Natadbasa Yate Suryona..."
61	Mohana	15	14	"Aham Vaiswanaro Bhutva..."
62	Rageshwari	5	18	"Vidyavinaya Sampanne....."
63	Rageshwari	7	9	"Punyogandhah Prudhivyam...."
64	Rageshwari	7	14	"Daivihyesha Gunamayee...."
65	Rageshwari	7	16	"Chaturvidhabhajante Mam..."
66	Rageshwari	5	23	"Shaknoti Haivayah Sodhum..."
67	Ragbairagbhairavi	11	32	"Kalosmin Lokakshaya Kruth Pravuddho Lokan...."
68	Ragbairagbhairavi	11	34	"Dronancha Bhishmancha Jayaradancha....."
69	Vakulabharanam	14	6	"Tatra Satvam Nirmalatva...."
70	Vijayanaagari	14	7	"Rajarogatmakam Viddi..."
71	Sankarabharanam	7	3	"Manushyanam Sahareshu"
72	Sankarabharanam	7	4	"Bhumiramonalo Vayuh..."
73	Sankarabharanam	7	7	"Mattahah Parataram Nanyat..."
74	Shuddhasaaveri	2	37	"Hatova Prapyasi Swargam...."

S. no	Ragas	Chapter	Sloka. no	Sloka
75	Shuddhasaaveri	2	47	"Karmanye vadhikaraste maa...."
76	Shubhapantuvarali	18	61	"Ishwara Sarva Bhootanam...."
77	Shubhapantuvarali	18	66	"Sarvadharman Parityajya....."
78	Shuddhasaranga	6	2	"Yam Sanyasamiti Prahuh...."
79	Shuddhasaranga	6	17	"Yuktahara Viharasya Yukta...."
80	Shuddhasaranga	6	19	"Yadhadeepo Nivatastho......"
81	Shanmukhapriya	16	21	"Trividham Naraka Syedam...."
82	Shanmukhapriya	16	23	"Yassastravidhi Mrut Srujya....."
83	Simhendramadhyamam	13	32	"Anadwitvannirgunatvat...."
84	Simhendramadhyamam	13	34	"Yatha Prakashayatyekah....."
85	Sindhubhairavi	2	62	"Dhyayato Vishayan Punsah..."
86	Sindhubhairavi	2	63	"Krodadbhavati Sammohah...."
87	Sindhubhairavi	18	2	"Kamyanam Karmanam Nyasam......."
88	Sindhubhairavi	18	12	"Anishta Mishtam Cha ......"
89	Sindhubhairavi	18	30	"Pravuttincha Nivruttincha..."
90	Sindhubhairavi	18	78	"Yatr Yogeshwar Krishno....."
91	Saudamini	14	4	"Sarva Yonishu Kaunteya...."

S. no	Ragas	Chapter	Sloka. no	Sloka
92	Hamir Kedar	10	30	"Prahladaschasmi Daityanam."
93	Hamir Kedar	10	41	"Yadyadwibhuti Mat atvam...."
94	Hamsadhwani	3	21	"Yadyadacharati Shreshtah.."
95	Hamsadhwani	3	30	"Mayi Sarvani Karmani....."
96	Hamsanandi	10	6	"Maharshayah Sap Purve...."
97	Hamsanandi	10	9	"Matchitta Madgata Pranah.."
98	Hindola	7	19	"Bhahunam Jnamanamanthe"
99	Hindola	8	5	"Antakalecha Mameva Smaran.."
100	Hindola	18	68	"Ya Idam Paramam Guhye.."
101	Hindola	18	72	"Kachchideta Chchrutam..."

Notes

1. T. M. Krishna, A Southern Music: The Karnatic Story Harper Collins, Publishers India, 201 *p*. 33
2. Ibid, *p*. 32
3. Mee Ghantasala, Ghantasala Atmakatha, *p*. 27
4. Ibid, *p*. 114
5. Ibid, *p*. 83
6. Ibid, *p*. 51
7. Ghantasala Jnapakalu, *p*. 197
8. Swaralahiri, *p*. 51
9. Ghantasala Jnapakalu, *p*. 106
10. Mee Ghantasala, *p*. 27
11. Ghantasala Jnapakalu, *p*. 13
12. A Southern music, *p*. 40.

13. Ibid, *p.* 42
14. K. Rohini *p*rasad, Sangeetam: Reetulu-Lotulu Hyderabad Book Trust, Hyderabad, 20 *p.* 4
15. A Southern Music, *p.* 104
16. From Ratnakumar's documentary on Ghantasala
17. Mee Ghantaala, Ghantasala Atmakatha, *p.* 27
18. Swaralahari, *p.* 51
19. S. V. Ramanamurthy gave me this information
20. Mee Ghantasala, *p.* 58
21. Ibid, *p.* 91
22. S. V. Ramanamurthy gave me this information
23. Ratnakumar Ghantasala suggested this point.
24. G. Gangadhara Shastry gave me this information
25. For preparing this roster of ragas, I took a lot of help from Sangeeta Rao, Asst. Director to Ghantasala, S. V. Ramana Murthy, Principal Annamachary Music College and author of the book 'Lavakusa' and Sivarama Prasad, author of 'E Ragamo, Idi E Ganamo'. Note that the ragas are given in Telugu alphabetical order.

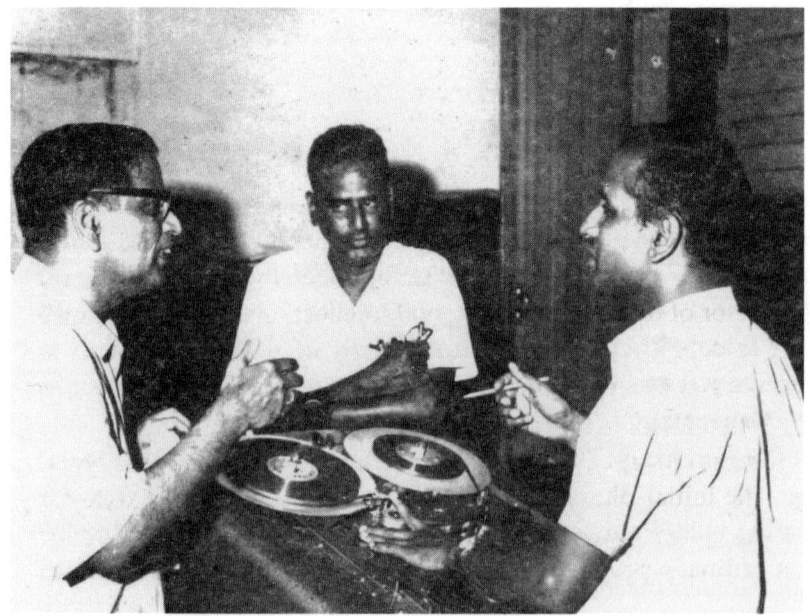

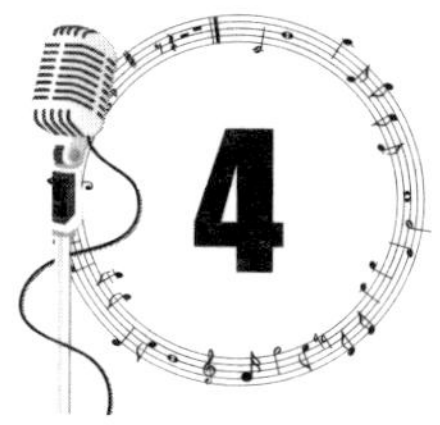

Enthralling Private Songs

Ghantasala sang a variety of private songs since 1946. Those songs can be divided into 8 categories:

A. Devotional songs
B. Classical songs
C. Light music
D. Folk songs
E. Patriotic songs.
F. Burrakathas
G. Yakshagana

A. **Devotional songs:**

Song 1: ***"Pujalandavayya Ganesha!... Jaya Gananatha! Jaya Gananatha!"***

Synopis: Oh Ganesha! Remove the problems and obstacles of human beings on the earth; likewise, have mercy on us and wipe off our sins: we will offer you the eatables like *'Kudumulu'* and *'Undrallu'*, in return bestow on us auspiciousness. As you are a protector of devotees, give us good intellect, make us do what we want to do without obstacles and endow us with the strength to perceive you everywhere. With piety, give us boons and protect us 'Jaya Gananatha'!

Commentary: This song was sung by Ghantasala in *'Kambhoja'* raga. The initial 'dha/sa/saa/sa/ri/dha/ swaras follow folk style for creating village atmosphere. The great composer made it easy for even ordinary people to sing it by arranging the two charanas to follow the same *'bani'* (style) and making the first two *'padas'* look similar.

Before the *'charana'*, 'counter' was beautifully used in the interlude. 'Counter' means to play or sing different *'swara'* combinations simultaneously in accordance with *'laya'* of the song. In this song bagpiper and violin instruments were used for 'Counter'. Ghantasala's innovative skills reflect here as he combined western style with the folk style of India.

The lyricist of the song was P. Venu and the record was released in 1962.

Song 2: *"Edukondala Saami Ekkadunnaavayya'... 'Neepaada Sannidhiki Mamu Jeraniyava"*

Synopsis: Oh! Venkatesa I have climbed hundreds of stairs; you are not seen; where are you? Oh! By staying on Tirumala Hill- which touches the skies – you wanted to keep the human beings at a distance. Learned men say that you are omnipresent; why can't I see you on this difficult path; Is it due to your *'Maya'*? I appeal to you to give your helping hand so that I can reach your Divine Feet!

This song was written Ravula Parti Bhadri Raju. He was the nephew of the well known writer Adavi Baapi Raju. His songs were sung by stalwarts like Ghantasala, S. Rajeshwara Rao, M. Balamurali Krishna, R. Balasaraswati Devi and P. Susheela. Ghantasala used *'Shuddha Dhanyasi'* raga for composing the song.

Commentary: The song yields multiple layers of meaning; it could be literal as well as metaphorical.

At literal level: It tells about an ordinary pilgrim, who starts walking on the stony path for reaching the pinnacle of the Seven Hills where Sri Venkateshwara Temple is situated. It talks about the physical difficulties faced by the pilgrim who is enervated and seeks the helping hand of the Lord of Seven Hills. While climbing the difficult steps, he ponders why the Lord is not seen who is supposed to be present everywhere. He, finally, appeals to the Lord to give him a helping hand so that he can reach the temple and see the divine feet.

At metaphorical level: A seeker, earning for the union with the Universal Soul, appeals to the Almighty (Varada) to wade him through the trials and tribulations of life. The stony path to the pinnacle indicates life's tough journey toward the ultimate goal.

Song 3: *"Namo Venkatesha! Namo Tirumalesha! ... Paramardham Telupavayya!"*

Synopsis: Salutation to you, Sri Venkatesha! Salutation to you, Oh Mahadevadeva! It is thrilling to greet you. By giving the offeringsto you, we fulfill our vows. By emancipating from our problems, please protect us. Make heaven out of the hell on earth. Show us the golden path for reaching and attaining *'Mukti'* (emancipation).

Commentary: The song *"Namo Venkatesha"* was also written by Ravula Parti Bhadri Raju. It is a sequel song to *"Edukondala Vaada"*. Ghantasala used *'Arabhi'* raga for composing this song. Metaphorically speaking offering one's hair and some amount of money are meant for getting rid of one's ego. By reducing the *'Arishat Varga'* (six enemies within), one will be closer to *'Mukti'* (emancipation)

Song 4: 'Venkanna Namame Bhakti To Kolichite... Oh Jeeva Chiluka Mukti Phala Mandudadaka'

Synopsis: If you worship Venkanna viz, Sri Venkateshwara, you will get rid of your sins, Oh parrot like soul! Introspection leads you to the path of devotion; the crucial cue for this is truthful life. Oh parrot like soul! Don't discrimate between mine and yours

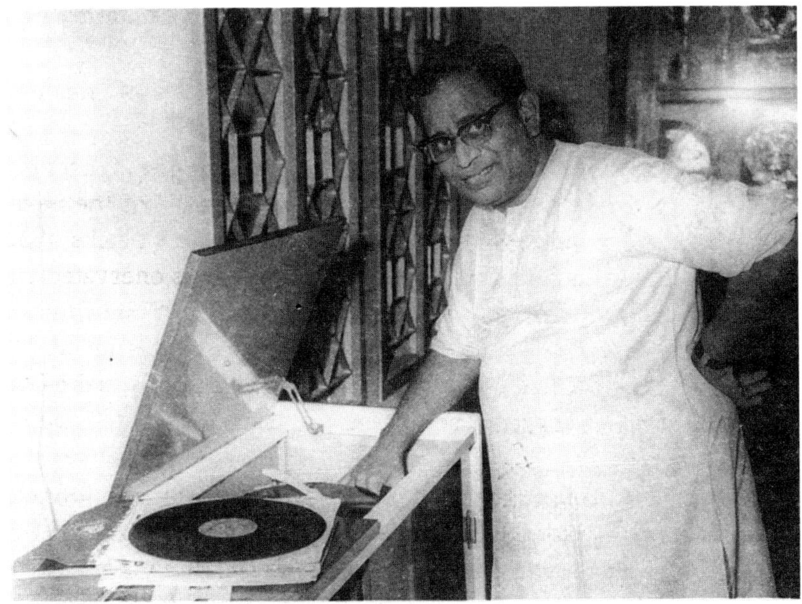

as it will lead you to misery; don't be egotistical. Take refuge at the feet of Venkanna! You will get salvation. Oh parrot like soul! Call the Lord of Seven Hills who is Lord of Lakshmi Devi; plead with Him to come fast for protecting his children. You will definitely get salvation.

Commentary: Even though the poet Ravi is less known, he expressions reflect not only the folk style but also indicate the easy way to attain salvation. An eloquent singer- composer like Ghantasala- whose voice contains, expresses and induces devotion- did ample justice to the lyrics as well as the poet. The singer-composer used 'Kambhoji' raga in 'Tisragati' for conveying the message. Instruments like the Ektara and Dholak were appropriately used for creating the folk atmosphere.

Song 5: 'Srisalamallanna! Melokovayya! ... Akasalinga-roopa! Akilalokaswaroopa! '

Synopsis: Oh Srisaila Mallikarjuna! Wake up for the sake of protecting your devotees. After crossing rivulets and rivers, hillocks and hills, we have reached you with hearts of devotion. Nandi (Bull) is your vehicle; serpents are your garlands. In the heart of Bhramaramba Devi that is Parvati Devi, your are beacon of gems. Shining like the blazing sun, you have taken the form of Jyotirlinga; in another place you are Prithvilinga; in the third place, you are

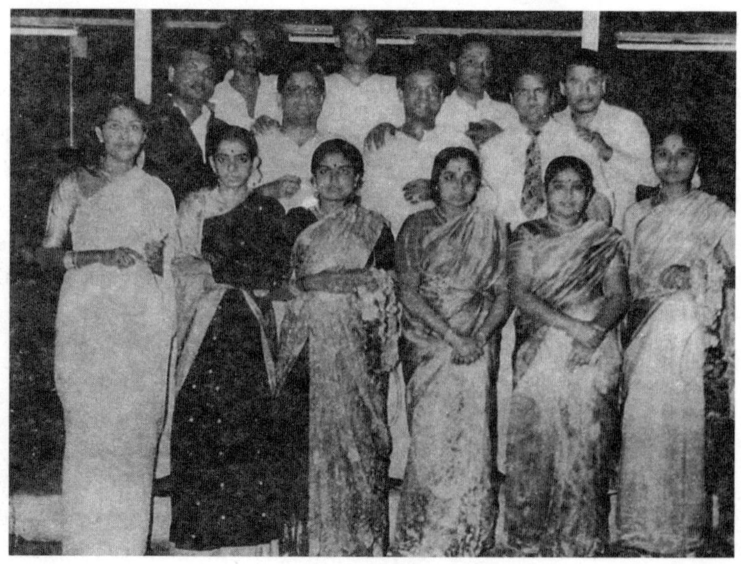

Apolinga; in the fourth place, you are Vayulinga; in the fifth place, you are Akashalinga. You are permeated in the entire universe. Salutations to you!

Commentary: Scholar poet C. Narayana Reddy wrote this song on Lord Shiva. At one place CNR mentioned that he had considered himself lucky as most of the songs written by him were sung by Ghantasala.

The music composer for this is Pandit Janardhan. He had been closely associated with Ghantasala since 1958 till 1974. Being a direct disciple of Pandit Ravi Shankar, he played the sitar in classics like 'Lava Kusa' and 'Rahasyam' and in the 'Ashtapadis', The Bhagavad Gita rendered by Ghantasala. For this song he used his favorite 'Chakravaka' raga. The 'gamakas 'used by Ghantasala were enthralling.

Song 6: 'Hey Mallikarjuna! Hey Bhakta Mandhara! ... Kanarandi Kannarandi Srisailamu'

Synopsis: Oh Mallikarjuna! Oh Lotus for the eyes of your devotees! It seems: you have accepted the worship of five Pandavas; you approved the services of Hema reddy; You showed mercy on Mallamma; The cresent is on your head and the mother of mothers is in your heart; she gave Shivaji the sword with which he killed his enimies; such a pilgrim cente, Srisailam will give salvation to every visitor, so people must visit that sacred place again and again.

Commentary: It is also a song written by C. Narayana Reddy and the composer is Pandit Janardhan. It has references to mythlogical and historical episode. The music composition comprises 'Ragamalika': 'Pahadi', 'Asaveri', Pantuvarali', 'Mohana' and 'Misra Malkauns – Chaturasragati' were used. As usual Ghantasala used his expertise to make it appealing. Both the song 5 and song 6 were written and composed for a documentary on 'Srisailam'. A gramphone recording company released the record.

B. Classical songs

Song 1: "Yaramita Vanamalina Sakhi... Pravisatu Hari-rapi Hridayamanena"

Synopsis: The lotus eyed Radha – who leads romantic life with the divine gardner Krishna – does not feel bad even if she has to sleep on a bed of leaves; the arrows of cupid cannot torment her;

the women who enjoyed the sweetness of the union with Krishna does not suffer from the prangs of separation from him.

Commentary: Sri Jayadeva lived in the 12th century near Puri of the present day Odisha. His magnam opus 'Geeta Govinda' contains 'Prabhandas'; The 'Prabhandas' contain couplets grouped into eights, called 'Ashtapadis'. There are 24 'Ashtapadis'. In an 'Ashtapadi', besides Pallavi and Anupallavi, there are 8 'Pada' or 'Charana'. The text also elaborates the eight moods of the heroine. The 'Ashta nayikas' have been an inspiration for many compositions and choreographic works in Indian classical dances. This is the 16th 'Ashtapadi' In 'Geeta Govinda' Radha stands for the individual soul and Sri Krishna stands for the universal soul. Ignoring the mundane world, if the individual soul pines for the union with universal soul, it (s/he) will not experience anguish or pangs of separation.

In the movie 'Bhakta Jayadeva' the music composer S. Rajeswara Rao used 'Bhimpalas' raga for composing the same 'Ashtapadi'. 'Bhimplas' – which belongs to Hindusthani music – is parallel to 'Abheri' raga of Carnatic music. In his private song Ghantasala used 'Abheri' raga for composing the same 'Ashtapadi'. The instruments the violin, the clarinet, the sitar, the flute and the table were appropriately used in the background.

Song 2: 'Dheera Sameere Yamuna Theere... Namate Sukrutha Kamaneeyam'.

Synopsis: On the shores of the river Yamuna slow breeze is making it pleasant. Sri Krishna, who has stolen the hearts of gopikas, is strolling over there. The flute player is good at loveplay also. Oh Radha with an enticing body! Follow your Krishna, says her friend.

Sri Jayadeva, who is an ardent devotee of Srihari, wrote enthralling 'Ashtapadis'.

Commentary: This is the 11th 'Asthapadi' in 'Geetagovinda'. Metaphorically speaking, Radha stands for the individual soul and Sri Krishna for the universal soul. An individual soul at a higher level of evolution wants to get united with the universal soul. In the movie 'Bhakta Jayadeva' S. Rajeswara Rao used 'Mohana' raga for composing this 'Ashtapadi'. Ghantasala in the private song used the same raga but sang in his own style(Bani).

Song 3: 'Yadi Hari Smrane Sarasam Mano... bhanati Jayadeva Kavi Raja Raje'

Synopsis: Preamble stanza: Listerners with discriminating abilities! If you want enjoy the praise of Lord Vishnu, If you are curious to listern to His Leela (play), focus on the sweet and enticing songs of Sri Jaya Deva.

O Radha with smiling face! Go fast for meeting Sri Krishna who is prancing up and down in the cottage made of creepers. There you will find the bed of Ashoka tree leaves. The entire atmosphere is permeated with the songs of cuckoo birds; then you enter the creaper cottage. When Sri Jayadeva along with Padmavathi sing songs in praise of Madhava, you join Sri Krishna and experience endless bliss.

Commentary: It is the 21st 'Ashtapadi in 'Geeta Govinda'. The preamble stanza 'Yedi Hari Smarane' was based on 'Kalyani 'raga. The same raga continued in the rest of the 'Ashtapadi' sung by singer – composer Ghantasala.

Song 4: 'Radhika Krishna Radhika... Sukhayathu Keshava Pada Mupaneetham'

Synopsis: O Keshava! Experiencing the pangs of separation from you, Radhika is not able to bear even the weight of the garland on her bosom; she even feels the weight of her thin body; she looks at the thick sandal paste as poison; she is meditating on Hari as though she is going to die. This song – which will give you pleasure – is dedicated to Keshava.

Commentary: This is the 9th 'Ashtapadi' in 'GitaGovinda'. In the magnum opus of Sri Jayadeva, there are two levels, physical and metaphorical; purusha and prakriti; yang and yin.

Song 5: 'Ramate Yamuna Pulinavana... Kavi Kripa Jaya-deva Ke'.

Synopsis: Sri Krishna stole the hearts of gopakantas while a gopakanta and he were strolling on the shores of Yamuna, Sri Krishna turned her face towards him for kissing it. In the moon-like the beautiful face of the gopakanta, he puts a sandalwood paste as a romantic sign.

Sri Jayadeva, who sings melodious songs in praise of Sri Hari, will not be touched by sin.

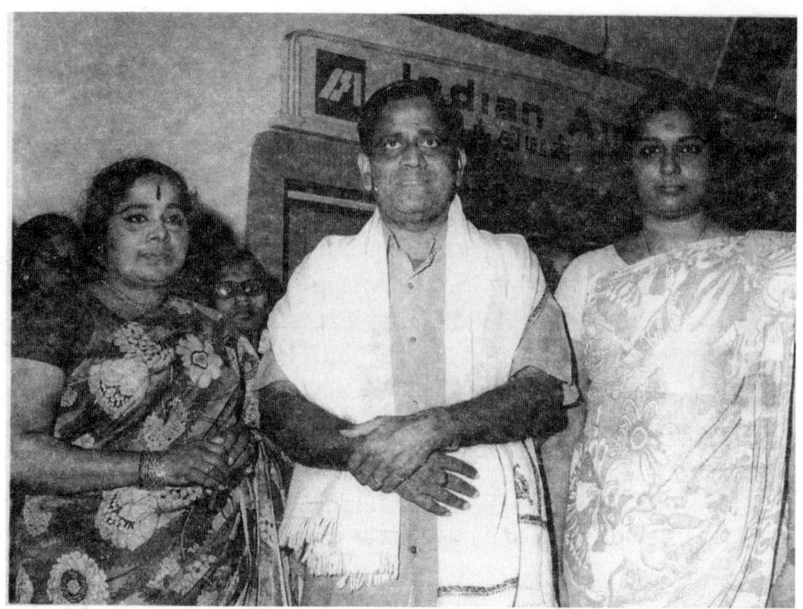

Commentary: It is the 15th 'Ashtapadi' in the epic 'Geetagovinda'. It is based on 'Peelu' raga of Hindustani tradition. Instruments like sitar and the flute were judiciously used by the singer-composer Ghantasala.

Song 6: 'Kshana Madhuna Narayanam... Rati Rasa Bhava Vinodam'.

Synopsis: Radha! Your beautiful feet are as fragile as flowers and as delicate as flesh leaves; they shame the flowers and the buds when you put your feet on the bed. I have now become Nari-Narayana. I have dried up due to the pangs of separation from you; give me life by giving the nectar of your lips.

May the songs of Sri Jayadeva in praise of Sri Hari give the persons with discriminating abilities the desire to attain him.

Commentary: It is the 23rd 'Ashtapadi' written by Sri Jayadeva and it was based on 'Gurjari Todi' raga of Hindustani Tradition. It was sung by Ghantasala over AIR in 1950. It was not recorded by AIR nor was it recorded by a recording company. It appears that a musician called Chittaranjan wrote the **Notation** for the song while listerning to it. Unnikrishnan-who is a classical musician – some how got the notation and the style (Bani) of Ghantasala and

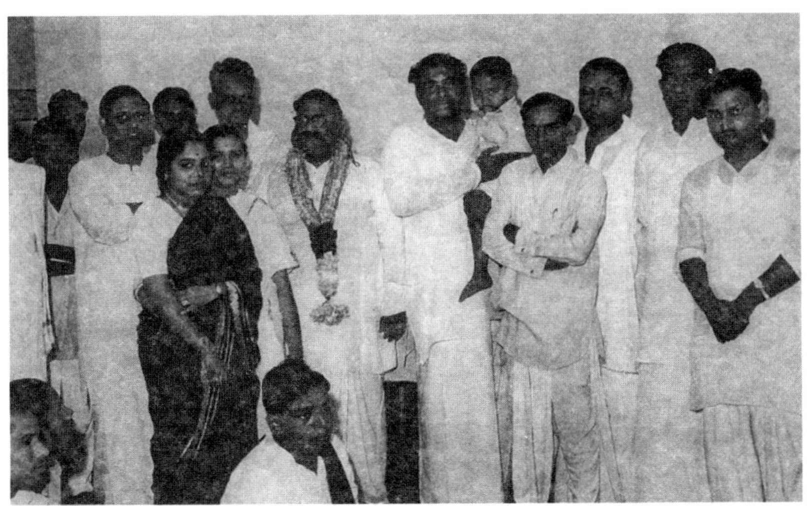

sang it melodiously. It is available in the CD called 'Sri Krishna Darshanam'.

Song 7: 'Brahma Kadigina Padamu... Parama Padamu Nee Padamu'

Synopsis: Your foot was cleansed by the creator Brahma himself; your foot itself is the Brahman. In the legend of king Bali, you occupied the earth, the sky and in accordance with the boons given to king Bali, you put your third foot on his head and pushed him to the nether world. Your foot washed off the sins of Ahalya; with your foot you danced on the head of Kaliya; with love your wife Lakshmi Devi presses it; Your chariot Garuda bears the weight of your foot: Your foot has the power to boons to the seers, the sages, and the saints; your foot indicates the direction to Tirumala for attaining salvation.

Commentary: This is a 'Keertana' of Annamacharya who lived in the 15th century. The music composer S. Rajeswara Rao used 'Hamsadwani' raga in 'Chaturasragati' for this song. Ghantasala sang it melodiously.

Song 8: 'Kolani Dopariki Gobbillo!... Kondalayyakunu Gobbillo! '

Synopsis: Salutations to the Lord of Yedukula who stole the robes and hearts of goppikas; who protected the villagers by lifting The Govardhanagiri; who punished the demons that visited

Brindavan; who killed Shisupala and Kamsa for making the people suffer; who is the Lord of seven hills.

Commentary: This is also a keertana written by Annamacharya. Ghantasala used 'Reeti Gaula' raga in 'Chaturasragati'. It was included in the long play record released in Newyork in 1971.

Song 9: 'Nanu Brovamani Cheppave Sitamma......Vela Nelataro Bhodhinchi'

Synopsis: O Sitamma! Will you please tell Sri Rama to save me? Your king Janaka's daughter, Janaki. Your are my mother. When you spend time with Sri Rama in a romantic manner, please tell him to protect me. When Sri Rama is waking up from sleep; please make him understand my situation.

Commentary: Bhakta Ramadasu was born in the 16th century. He was known for his ardent devotion to Sri Rama and his keertanas' in praise of Sri Rama. His Keertanas' are suffused with meliflous Telugu words. Even Tyagaraja had a lot of admiration for Bhakta Ramadasu. Eventhough Ramadasu- the author of this keertana- has appealed to Sri Rama number of times. He has not responded. Using the Sanskrit saying 'Kanta Sadrusham', he pleads with mother Sita to represent his case to her husband Sri Rama when he is in a romantic mood. Alternatively, she may plead Ramadas's case with Sri Rama when he has had a full night sleep and just waking up.

In his rendition, Ghantasala followed folk style and used 'Bilahari' raga. The song was included in the long play record released in Newyork in 1971.

Song 10: 'Chalamelara Saketha Rama... Thalajalara Tyagaraja nutha'

Synopis: O Rama! Why are you laconic with me? Having loved you and admired you, I have been describing you in accordance with the path of devotion. Seeking your favour where shall I go? What shall I do? Who should I appeal to? I cant' spend my time just by singing long ragas. I cant' bear this any more, O Saketa Rama.

Commentary: Tyagaraja, Muthu Swami Dixitar and SamaSastry were the Trinity – The three illustrious 'Vaggeyakaras' of carnatic music. Of them Tyagaraja was born in the 18th century. This keertana is based on 'Margahindola' raga in adi tala. Ghantasala meticulously followed the same. This was also included in the long play record released in New York. Descerning leaders/listerners can see the similarities between this keertana and the previous keertana of Bhadrachala Ramadasu.

Song 11: 'Samajavaragamana... Vinoda Mohanakara! Tyagaraja Vandaneeya'

Synopsis: Oh, Sri Rama! You saunter like a royal elephant. You make the lotus-hearts of the saints' blossom. Your qualities are praised by means of nectar – like music born out of Vedas. Oh Narayana with a merciful heart! Protect me. You shine like the light placed on the pinnacle made of the seven swaras which originated from Samaveda. Oh, Murali Krishna of Yadava clan! Salutations to you!

Commentary: It is a popular keertana of Tyagaraja who used 'Hindola' raga in 'Adi' tala. Ghantasala scrupulously followed Tyagaraja. He sang it in Calcutta and Washinton DC.

The music composer for this is Pandit Janardhan. He had been closely associated with Ghantasala since 1958 till 1974. Being a direct disciple of Pandit Ravi Shankar, he played the sitar in classics like 'Lava Kusa' and 'Rahasyam' and in the 'Ashtapadis', The Bhagavad Gita rendered by Ghantasala. For this song he used his favorite 'Chakravaka' raga. The 'gamakas' used by Ghantasala were enthralling.

C. Light music

Song 1: ***"Pushpa Vilapam"***

'Eko Rasah! Karunah!', proclaimed the Sanskit poet and playwright, Bhavabhuthi. The Telugu poet Papaiah Shastri and the mesmerizing singer – composer Ghantasala make the discerning listeners of the master pieces – *"Advaita Murti"*, *"Sandhyasri"*, *"Pushpa Vilapam"* and *"Kunti Kumari"*- feel that *'Karuna'* is the only rasa. *"Advaita Murti"* and *"Sandyasri"* were recorded in 1949. On both sides of 78 RPM record, 6 stanzas of *"Pushpa Vilapam"* were recorded in 1950. All the stanzas were composed on the basis of Hindustani ragas.

The first stanza: *"Nenoka Poola Mokka Kada Nilchi... Thalukumanadi Pushpa Vilapa Kavyamai"*

Ghantasala used *'Maand'* raga for the rendition of this stanza. In the audio, the adept composer created the atmosphere of early morning in a garden where the presence of a temple and pooja for the Lord were clearly perceived by the listeners. *'Alapana'* was precise and dignified.

The next stanza: *"Aayuvu Galgu Naalgu Ghadiyalu'... Aayama Challani Kali Vellapai"*

The rendition of this stanza was based on *'Maru bihar'* raga.

The following stanza is *"Gaalini Gauravintumu... Thalini Bidhanu Veru Chethuve"*

Ghantasala used *'Basant'* raga for composing this stanza. The right 'rasa' pathos was permeated throughout the rendition. It would tell about the skill of the composer in making the raaga serve his purpose.

The following sarcastic stanza runs like this: *"Oolu Daralatho Gonthu...... Akata Daya Leni Varu Mee Adavaru"*

Ghantasala used *'Pahadi'* raaga for the rendition of this stanza.

The next stanza *"Ma Velaleni Mugdha Sukumara...Kadaa nara Jathiki Neetiunnada?"*

The raga *'Misra Sivaranjani'* suited this stanza as it reflected *'Karuna Rasa'* (pathos)

The final stanza – *"Buddhadevuni Bhoomilo.....Nee Manuja Janma"*, was based on *'Raagesri'* raga.

By using suitable raga, appropriate background music, poetic prose in between and meaningful expression, Ghantasala made *'Pushpa Vilapam'* remain in the hearts of lakhs of people.

Song 2: *"Kunthi Kumari"*

It was written by Jandhyala Papaiah Shastry in 1951. Ghantasala composed music for it and sang it. The record came out in 1953.

Synopsis: The long poem – comprising a number of stanzas-describes how an unmarried princess called Kunti gives birth to her son and how she leaves the baby in the Ganga after putting him in a box.

Commentary: Toeing the line of his guru, Patrayani Seetarama Shastry, Ghantasala did not undermine the *'Sahitya'* (literature) part of the poem; he made the meaning and mood of every word or sentence that manifested in the composition; having got the expertise in classical ragas, Ghantasala knew how to use *'Sahitya'* effectively and how to create new ragas and make them serve his purpose. He edited the long poem written by 'Karunasri' and used his meaningful prose commentary in praise of the stanzas taken out.

The first stanza: *"Adi Oka Ramaniya................Kriniki Metlamidugaa"*

Ghantasala used *'Khamas'* raga for composing this stanza.

The second stanza: *'Kanniya Laanti Valakamu............ Yanaradhata Dame Biddaye'*

This stanza is based on *'Mand'* raga (but *'Madhyamam'* appears in between). For guiding the listeners – cursory as well as discerning-and creating dramatic effect, the skillful composer gives the signpost in *'vachanam'* (prose): *'Aame Santhosha Paduthunnada Leka Dhukkapaduthunnada'* (Is she happy or is she sad?)

The third stanza: *'Doralu Ananda.................Muddu Chekkutaddameeda'.*

The raaga used for this stanza was *'Hindolam'*. Even though the swaras in 'hindolam' raga are 'sa/ga/ma/dha/ni/sa, sa/ni/dha/ma/ga/sa', Ghantasala had the habit of using *'Pachamam'* in this raga.

(The next stanza written by the poet was not taken by Ghantasala as the adept singer-composer wanted to keep the focus on Kunti Kumari.)

Before the beginning of the following stanza- when the listeners are wondering who the 'Lady with the Baby' is- Ghantasala comes out with another signpost: *'O Ho Telisindi'* (O I have come to know) the stanza reads like this: *'Gaali Thakuna Jalatharu.......Sukumari Aame Kunthi Kumari'.* **With this the first side of the first 78RPM record was over.**

In the second side the first stanza reads like this: *'Muni Mantrammu..........Kunthi Swobhagyamul'.*

During the visits of Bade Ghulam Ali Khan to Madras in the late 1940s and later, Ghantasala became an admirer and a friend of the great Hindustani singer. Being a receptive mind, the young singer learnt a number of Hindustani ragas from the senior singer. One of the ragas is *'Raagesri'*. Ghantasala made use of this raga for rendering the present stanza.

The next stanza written by the poet was not used by Ghantasala in his version. Instead, the signpost *'Ayyo Bhagavanuda'* (Oh God) was used.

It is followed by the stanza: *"Ee Vishada Shruvulathoda............ Kanna Kaduputhoda"* - it is based on *'Mayamalavagaula'* raga.

Instead of the next five stanzas written by the poet, Ghantasala, in his version, comes out with musical, precise and profound *'vachanam'* (prose):

"Ee Vidhanganischayinchukuni—Nadi Tarangalalo Telutu------Eshwarechcha----Petteninduga----Prakkameeda Chitti Tandrini Bajjunda Bette Talli"

The first 78 RPM record ended here.

The first side of the second 78 RPM record starts with the stanza: *"Bhogabhagyalatho -----Pettikonochanaithi Papishti Daana."* The adept composer used *'Amruthavarshini'* raga for composing this stanza.

Instead of the following stanza written by the poet, Ghantasala used the expression *"Naa Chittibabu!"(*My little darling!)

The next stanza *"Pettiyalona Notthigilapetti---------Ninubolina Ratnam Naaku Dakkune"*

Ghantasala used *'Shubhavanthuvarali'* (Hindustani *'Todi'* for composing this stanza.

This was followed by Ghantasala's meaningful expression *"Ayyo Tandri!"* (Oh, darling baby!)

The next stanza *"Punnma Chandamama------------Maatagadoyi Naayana" 'Hemavathi'* raga was used by the composer for this stanza.

The following two stanzas written by the poet were left out by the skillful composer.

Instead he used the expression *"Talli Gangabhavani*!"(Mother Ganga!) as a signpost.

The next stanza is *"Balabhanunibolu-------Namastulamma! Namastulamma!"* The adept composer started this with *'Peelu'* raga and effortlessly slid into *'Sindhubhairavi'* raga.

The next stanza is *"Marulu Rekettha Biddanu-----------Pettelopalanunchi Jokotte Talli!"*

The raga used was *'Gunkali'* raga which is Hindustani raga and the inspiration was Bade Ghulam Ali Khan. Ghantasala's expression *"Aame Mathru Hridayal Thata Thata Kottu Kunnnadi Papam"* (A mother's love for the baby makes Kunti's heart palpitations increase.)

The rest of the stanzas were composed by using *'Lalit'* raga.

The next stanza is *"Atha Pathram Bhangi Sanjatha Pathrammu"----Neeti Loniki Drose Pette"*

Then Ghantasala's *'vachanam'*describes the scene': *"Nadi Tarangalalo Pette Kottukoni Pothunnadi"* (The box is wading through the waves of the Ganga)

The last stanza is *"Eti Keratallalo Pette Eguchunda ----Lochanamulatho Kunti Chuchuchununde."*

In the backdrop of orchestra comprising Hawaiian guitar and other instruments; Ghantasala-simulated Kunti Kumari cries wih intensity:

"Babu, Babu, Naa Nanna Naa Nanna!" (My darling! My darling! My baby! My baby!) The orchestra creates the dramatic climax which was astounding.

In both the 78 RPM records, one can hear the pleasant music of Hawaiian guitar.

Song 3: *"Aa Rajini Kara Mohana Bimbam......Tala Ninda Pudanda Dalchini Raani.......Nee Nelaveni Loo Niliche Akashalu"*

Synopsis: Oh My queen! Can I compare yor smiling face with the enticing moon? Or the blooming lotuses comparable to your bewitching eyes? Wherever I see, wherever I wait, you appear before me. With your head decked with flowers and with your budding smiles, don't try to enthrall me. Are you a cloud which showers flowers? Are you the charm, in screwpine leaves? In the path of your words, there are hibiscus flowers; In the garden of your songs, romance (sringara) is blooming; your body is suffused with beauties of chrysanthemum flowers; in your black plait, the skies are hidden.

Commentary: This poem was written by a famous poet Dasarathi. The poet described the typical attitude of a lover pining for the embrace of his beloved: he wondered whether her smiling face was comparable with the moon, her eyes with the blooming lotuses; he saw her everywhere; he noticed all kinds of flowers associated with her; he visualized her head decked with flowers; she like a cloud raining flowers; her words, her songs and her entire body full of flowers.

The poet Dasarthi used a few metaphors:

1. The beloved smiling face was compared to the moon;
2. Her beautiful eyes were compared to the blooming lotuses;
3. The lover observed that the path of her words was suffused with hibiscus flowers; the garden of her songs was full of romance and love; her body was permeated with the chrysanthemum flowers; her plait looked like the skies.

The song described the typical attitude of a lover who is obsessed with the beauty of his beloved; since he is obsessed, he comes out with a number of metaphors.

The adept singer composer, Ghantasala used his favorite *'Kalyani'* raga, and it was in *'Chaturashra Gati'* appropriate for this romantic song. His modulations while describing the charms of the beloved are amply indicative of the obsession of the lover. While singing the first stanza about the cloud that would rain flowers, the singer went to *'Tara Sthayee Shadjam'* indicating the height of the cloud and immediately came down to *'Madhyama Sthayee Nishadam'*. Again while referring to Akashalu (skies), he used *'Shadjam'*.

Song 4: *"Veliginchave Chinni Valapu Deepam……Aa Deepamunnacho Naa Kemi Lopam"*

Synopsis:

He says: My beloved! Why don't you light a beacon of love? Why so much of anger against me?

She responds: There is a golden beacon in the mind; if it is not lit, it's a sin.

He says: The red dot on your face is my beacon; if I look at it, my desire increases.

She responds: I see a beacon of love in your eyes; when it is there, there is inadequacy.

He says: In the palace of sky there is beacon; if it is estinquished, it will be curse for the earth.

She responds: Look! The beacons of stars are giving light to the world.

He says: If there is beacon of love in your heart, there is no shortcoming.

Commentary: This is a sequel song to "Talaninda Poodanda" and also written by Dasarthi. The record was released in 1965.

'Telang' raga and *'Jhampa tala'* was used by the singer – composer for the song. As he left the end words of the song – *'Taapam, Shapam and Lopam'* – at *'Tara Sthayee Panchamam'*, it became a smooth path for him to go on to *'Pallavi'* – *'Veleginchave Chinni Varapu Deepam'*

In the song the voice of the male was that of Ghantasala and female was that of P. Leela. In this song also Dasarathi used a few metaphors: intense love compared to a golden beacon; vermillion dot compared to a light. This song refects the romantic notions of lovers.

Song 5: *"Phakkuna Neevu Navvina........Kalasi Melasi Manasulu Murise Kapuramachate pettenu"*

Synopsis:

He says: If you smile wholeheartedly, all your beauties will be visible

She responds: If you are with me the entire universe smiles

He says: Even if you are in a big crowd, my eyes will locate you

She responds: As you are the man of my desire, my mind forces me to go to you

He says: If I look at your shining body, time stands still (for me)

She responds: Even if I spend a little time with you, it gives me the nectar for sustaining

He says: Beyond the skies, I have built a palace of hope

She responds: There we will live together to the rejoicement of our minds and senses

Commentary: The song was written by Arudra who was a scholar-poet.

The tune for the song was based on *'Madhyamavati'* raga *'Ata thala'*. As the song was long the *'Pallavi'* was not repeated. Ghantasala's was the male voice and P. Leela's the female voice.

Song 6: *"Paadake Naa Rani Paadake Paata ----Paadala Gathulu Nrityammate"*

Synopsis: Oh, my queen! Don't sing my darling! The sweetness of your song, makes me hot. If you sing your raga surrounds me like a rivulet and makes me disappear in the waves. When your lips-which are like the buds of *'Sougandhika Pushpam,'* imprison me with mantras like romantic words. My mind is not tuned to your melodious songs; can one dance who does not know how to walk?

Commentary: The song was written by a famous poet and novelist called Adavi Bapiraju. The adept singer-composer used *'Aasaravi'* raga, *'Jhampa thala'* of Hindustani tradition. Meaningful metaphors were used by the knowledgeable poet, Adavi Bapi Raju.

Raga was aptly compared to a rivulet; in a raga, there are waves just like in a rivulet.

i. Buds of *'Sougandhika'* were compared to the lips of a woman.

ii. Words of love or romance were compared to mantras.

iii. This song also tells us how a lover pines for his beloved.

Song 7: ***'Bahudhurapu Batasari... Neeto Goni Povoyi'***

Synopsis: Oh long distance traveler! Please come this way. Why do you want to travel at midnight? It 's cyclonic weather. This is my cottage; come and rest for a while; you can leave early morning. Which is your destination? Are you going to your country? You take me along with you; we will go together.

Commentary: The song was written by Ghantasala himself. There is dramatic backdrop to this. It seems one night while the singer-composer was standing in the balcony of Sobhanachala Studios, he saw a dead body being carried by some men with petromax lights. Some say that the sight inspired Ghantasala to write the song; also, they say that the preamble to the song shoud also be considered.

As the multi-talented writer was a genius, we can expect the song to yield layers of meaning.

Layer 1. Death- like a seasoned traveler travels long distances. An individual soul does not want to leave the body (here the cottage); at midnight - which symbolizes untimely death. She wants death to take her with him after the sunrise as by then all her desires/wishes will be fulfilled. (If the individual soul was Ghantasala, his appeal was not considered by death as the singer-poet faced untimely death.)

Layer 2. Another anecdote leads us to a different layer of interpretation. As one side of 78 RPM record had *"Bahudoorapu Batasari"*, the singer - composer's assistant suggested that another

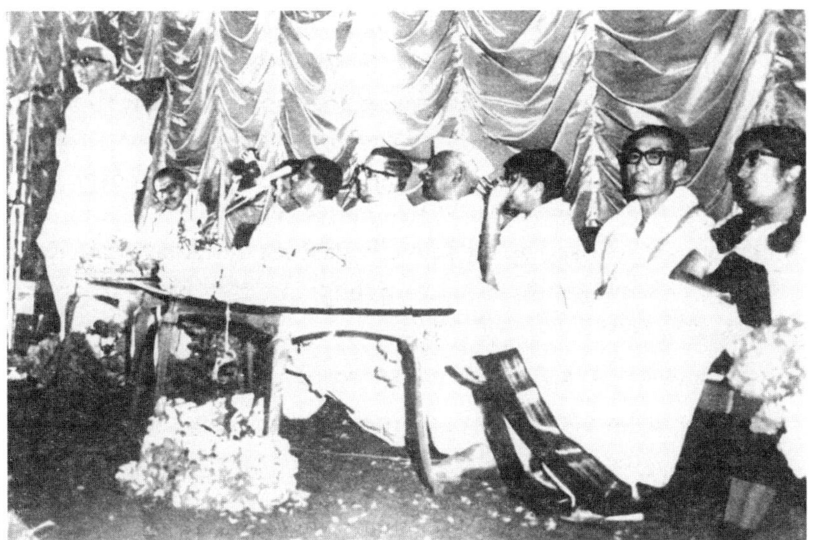

song written by Ghantasala viz., *"Marana Samayamidiye"* could be recorded on the second side; the wise poet-singer told him that those songs would not match each other and that *"Ravoyi Bangari mama"* should be recorded.

The 78 RPM record containing *"Bahudoorapu Batasari"* and *"Ravoyi Bangari Mama"* was released sometime in1951-52.

Among *'Ashtanayikas'* of Bharata's *'Natyashastra',* two 'Nayikas' namely, *'Proshitabhatruka'* (one with a sojourn husband) and *'Abhisarika'* (one who moves) come close to the woman described in *"Bahudoorapu Batasari"* who calls the traveler-may be her husband on sojourn-to come into the cottage, rest for a while and continue the journey the following morning as the climate is cyclonic and the time is midnight; in a persuasive manner, she tells him that if he comes to her cottage, her desires will be fulfilled and that he might as well take her with him.

The singer-composer used his favorite *'Kalyani'* raga in *'Thisragati'* for composing the song. Before the preamble, instuments like piano, violin and shehnai were judiciousy used.

Song 8: *"Naavika echati koyi nee payanam--------nee vechati koyi"*

Synopsis: Oh. Seafarer! Where are you going? Immediately after sunrise, you left behind your beloved. Which shores will you approach? Which island will you reach? You don't even look straight at me even though you are like th thousand-rayed Sun. Why don't you take your beloved too. Both can go together hand in hand. In the mid sea when the tides are high, you are going on a rudderless ship. Where are you going? Where are you going?

Commentary: The name of the writer is not given, but a stylistic analysis of the song tells us that the song was written by Ghantasala and that it was fit to be a sequel to Bahudurapu Batasari. Layer 2 interpretation of Bahudurapu Batasari is apt for this song also. The beloved who calls the seafarer is a 'Proshitabhatruka' (One whose husband is on a sojourn) The adept singer-composer used 'Keeravani'raga in 'Chaturasragati' The instruments the Veena, the Vilolin, the Flute and the Clarinet were melodiously used.

Song 9: 'Repulo maapulo chupu nilipedavela ---- Le levoy Ashajeevi --- swarasargapu nirmananiki'

Synopsis: "Don't keep your eyes on tomorrow for doing things. Oh, Optimist! Wakeup and come up! You can bring down the lighning; you can teach the worlds how to walk; you can quickly control even the thunderbolts; you can show a beacon of light to the people of the world.

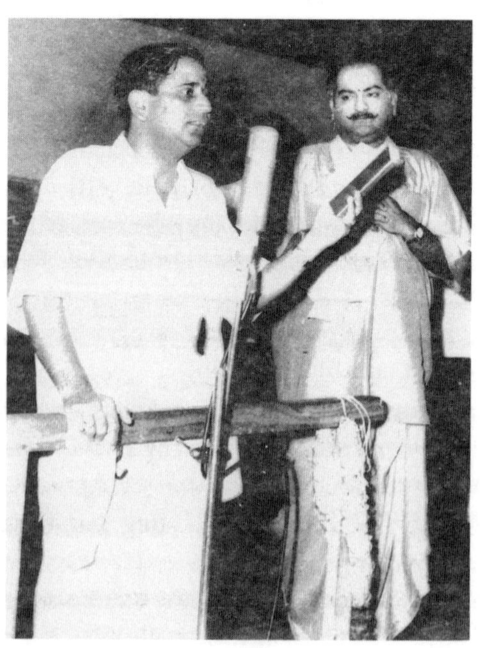

Commentary: This song was written by Tholeti Venkata Reddy. It is an inspirational song wherein we can clearly see the influence of Mahakavi Sri Sri. Also, it reminds us of the clarion call of Swami Vivekananda: "Arise! Awake! Stop not till the Goal is reached." The singer-composer deftly used 'Maund'raga in 'chaturasragati.' for composing the song. The instrumental music was appropriately used for enhancing the beauty of 'Maund'raga.

Song 10: "Le levoy Ashajeeva.......... Swarasargapu Nirmananiki"

Synopsis: O, Optimist! Wake up and come up! You can bring down the lightning; you can teach the worlds how to walk; you can show a beacon of light to the worlds; self – centeredness is killing the society in an insidious manner; don't become a prey to it. Try to destroy the dominance by a few; Try to empower the poor; Try for the weal and welfare of the entire humanity; Try to build united voice of the people.

Commentary: This song was written by Tholeti Venkata Reddy. It is an inspiring song where in we can clearly see the influence of Maha Kavi Sri Sri. Also, it reminds us of the clarion call of Swami Vivekananda "Arise! Awake! Till the goal is reached".

The singer-composer deftly used 'Maund' raga in 'Chaturasra gati' for composing the song. The instrumental music was appropriately used for enhancing the beauty of 'Maund' raga.

D. Folk Songs:

Song 1. Preamble: 'Pasidi polalalo palle paduchu thana mama kosam kalavara paduthu ila pilustondi' (A village belle in love with her close relation expresses her feelings through this song)

"Raavoyi Bangari mama --- mana vagal kalabosikundamu"

Synopsis: Oh. my darling relation! I want to share a secret with you. Water drops, it seem, are singing a song; when I hear I heart palpitation increases. Two flowers are too high forme; you pluck them and arrange them in my plait. While going on the river, we will listen to the boatsman's song and share sweet nothings with each other.

Commentary: The writer of the song was Konakalla Venkata Ratnam. The singer-composer used 'Bhimplas' raga for this song. The attitude of a typical villagebelle is described in this song. The language used is pure Telugu for expressing the feelings of the village girl.

Song 2: 'Attha leni kodalutthamuralu o lamma---manchi-dani malle malli poyindi ahum ahum'

Synopsis: Prelude: Mother in law (Mil) without Daugher in law (Dil) is very good; Dil without Mil virtuous

Mil: My son's wife! Where is the cream in the fresh milk? Where is the butter in the hot milk?

Dil: Stop your tantrums, Mil! Can there be cream in the fresh milk? Can there be butter in the hot milk?

Mil: its okhay. What happened to the laddus kept in the hanging pot?

Dil: When we have a big cat like you in the house, who can dare eat them

Mil: You go, foul tongue!

Commentary: It is a typical folk song. The adept singer-composer used dramatic techniques while rendering the song. He appropriately played the roles of Mil and Dil and created a lot of subtle humor. The main song was composed in 'Mohana' raga Madhyama shruti' and for the background music 'Kuranji'raga 'Madyama Shruti' was used. Even though the lyrics formed part of Telugu tradition, the 2nd and 3rd stanzas were written by Samudrala Raghavacharya. This song is one of the most popular songs of Ghantasala.

Song 3: 'Panchadaravanti police Venkatasaami----manaku sandaamama thodu'

Synopsis: Oh, Police Venkataswamy! You are as sweet as sugar. I can't forget your inviting eyes. You have got nascent mustache, I have recently reached ripe age. If our hearts are united, we need not fret about other things. Your eyes and my eyes have met; you and I have met. Hither or thither. I 'm your shade. I can never forget you: you are mine and I am yours. If the the Moon plays witness, there is no separation between you and me. We are one.

Commentary: As in 'Ravoyi Bangari mama', the beloved's yearning for her lover is reflected in this song also. Her anxiety, her desire and her eagerness are clearly shown in word-pictures. To paraphrase a playback singer cum critic of the stature of P. B. Srinivos, in Ghantasala' s voice every lilt and nuance, all the contours and charms of a village belle were clearly palpable. He added that when the adept singer-composer sang this song in a typical folk-style in a concert, every male listener felt that he was 'Police Venkatasaami' The singer-composer used a pure classical raga like 'Hari Khamboji' and made it so simple that even lay persons like villagers loved to sing this song. The flute, the clarinet, and the violin were used for producing enthralling background music.

E. Patriotic songs

Song 1: 'Swatantrayame maa janma hakkani... mangalyapu haratu limma'

Synopsis: Proclaimed to the world that Freedom is our Birthright! Fearlessly fight with despotic forces! There is no difference between life and death, if you are alivebut a slave. With the fires of warm blood, wage freedom struggle! Even if you are tolerant for along time, the plunderers will not become merciful. Following the path of peace and non violence, unite the people fast.

Commentary: "Freedom is My Birth Right," proclaimed Bala Gangadhar Tilak, the leader of leaders. That was clarion call to the nation against the Britsh. The author of the song, Toleti Venkata Reddy used this clarion call for writing an inspiring song. The singer composer Ghantasala used 'Bhimplas' raga in 'Chaturasagati'. In the background he appropriately used the clarinet, violin and trumpet indicating a battle with demonic forces.

Song 2: "Le lendoy ra randoy... haddulu daati poye-varaku"

Synopsis: Wake up and Come, Get up and Come Oh, Indians! Oh, Warriors! Pandit Nehru believed in India China brotherhood. The expansionistic and demonic Chinese smeared the belief unscrupously. The principle of love and non violence propounded by Gautama the Buddha and the universe's message of peace have no impact on the Chinese; they have blood – thirsty. Be patriotic; give bountiful contributions and gold; donate your blood. Forgetting the differences of caste and creed and remaining united, we should make Chinese flee from our borders.

Commentary: Ghantasala was not only a good Gandhian, but also a patriot to the core of his personality. After the Chinese aggression had taken place in 1962, the singer-composer along with a team of actors like NT Rama Rao and A. Nageswara Rao plunged into action and collected funds for the Defence fund of Government of India. This song is the one of the inspiring patriotic songs sung by Ghantasala.

This was written by an unknown poet called N. Anjibabu. The singer – composer used 'Hindola' raga for composing the patriotic song. Along with the Indian instruments, a western instruments like 'side drums' was also used for creating the atmosphere of a battle.

Song 3: "Amma Sarojini Devi!... Amrutamu Chinditivamma"

Synopsis: Oh, Sarojini Devi, you are our mother! You are the jewel among women; You are like a branch of a shrub of roses. Your poems are like the songs of a cuckoo bird. You plunged into the freedom struggle with your sword like pen. You life history is as pleasant as a love story. With your love and affection, you gave nectar to the people of India.

Commentary: After the demise of Sarojini Naidu, Tholeti Venkata Reddy wrote this song and Ghantasala sang it sonorously. It's a melodious tribute paid to the Nightingale of India. The song was composed on the basis of 'Sindhubairavi' raga in 'Chaturasragati'.

Song 4: "Andhurla Charitam Ati Rasabharitam.... Desa Desamula Minchandoy"

Synopsis: Oh, Andhras i.e. Telugu speaking people! If you listen to the history of Telugus, you hearts will beat faster. The courage of Tanguturi, the tenacity of Bulusi, the bravery of Venkatagiri and the former-friend Ranganayakulu keep the history of Telugus alive forever. Ignoring the differences of caste and creed, if all the Telugus join their hands together, our fame will reach the zenith. Instead of uttering words, let us show it in action that we love our country. The nation is not just made of land but the people too. Let us raise above other countries.

Commentary: This song was also written by Tholeti. The singer-composer Ghantasala used 'Mishra Sankarabharana' raga. The tune has some similarities with 'Mand' raga.

F. Burra Katha

Song: "Venara Bharata Veera Kumara Vijayam Manadera.... Chinamookanu Tharamali"

Synopsis: Listern! Oho, Indian warriors! Be prepared to protect your country; it is yours. Aggressive Chinese have damaged the piece of our country. Understand that we are in trouble!

Question: But why the Chinese have attacked us? You say why. The reason is: Our country is progressing fast with heavy industries, dams across the rivers, atomic energy centres, five year plans and 'Panchayati' local government system. Our country is contributed to the freedom of the countries which are lagging behind; As a result, we are getting good reputation among the Asian and African countries. Be jealous of our reputation, they stabbed us in the back. They talked about the path of truth, 'Panchsheel', The Buddha, Gandhi and the brotherhood of Indians and Chinese; of singing the lullaby, they stabbed us in the back. Thus they opened our eyes. As the Chinese had their eyes on Ladakh and NEFA, our soldiers got into action; they climbed snow clad mountains; they crossed thick forests; they were not afraid of Pathan tanks. The USA and UK came to our help by providing the latest arms.

Question: So when our defence forces were waging a bitter battle, what should the civilians do? From every family, there should be a representative in the Army or The Navy or The Airforce. Till the clouds of war disappear, farmers, factory workers and labourers should work very hard with determination and tenacity; they should increase production and contribute to economic development: women should give up gold jewellery; wasteful expenditure should be avoided; frugality should be cultivated; they should contribute to the defence fund for strengthening the hands of our military forces. The Chinese should be driven out; they should be thrown out.

Commentary: In Telugu culture there is a genre called Burra katha. It is an oral story telling technique, in the Katha tradition, performed in the villages of the two Telugu states. The troupe consists of one main performer and two co performers. The subject will be a mythtological story or a historical story or a socio-polital issue. 'Burra' refers to Tambura and 'Katha' means story. The famous poet Pingali – who wrote songs for many of the Vijaya Productions like 'Patalabhairavi',- wrote this song also. The singer- composer used 'Mohana' raga in 'Trisra gati' and at times in 'Chaturasra Gatti'. Instruments like the drums and the trumpet were appropriately used. P. Susheela, P. Leela, Madhavpeddi and J. V. Raghavulu were the supporting singers.

After Chinese aggression in 1962, Ghantasala with his team comprising NTR went to different parts of the country for collecting funds. In that situation this inspiring song was used.

G. Yakshgana

Song: 'Girija Kalyanam': "Jaya jaya nataraja! Rajatashailavasa! ..... Sri Venugopala! Jaya Magalam! Trailokya Mandhara! Subhamangalam!"

Synopis: Oh, Nataraja! Himashala is your house and serpents are your ornaments. You are an embodiment of Bhava- Raga- Tala. Parvati occupies half of your body. The angels worship you. Salutations to you Parvatidevi! Oh, Parameshwari! Your beautiful hair moves when the breeze comes from hills. Salutations to you Oh, Mother of Kartikeya! 'Bahuparak' to Ganapati who has blessings of Uma and Maheshwara! 'Bahuparak' to Kumara Subramanya who is known for his prowess of shoulders! 'Bahuparak' to Magaladri Narasimha, Mother of mothers Kanakadurga, and Kuchipudi Venugopala!

Signpost: The Yakshgana narrates how Shiva's anger turns Manmatha into ashes and how Shiva, after understanding the intensity of Parvati's love, marries her and revives Manmatha.

Narration: Her close friends ask Parvati Devi where the female Swan was going: she responded by saying that she is going to meet her king Swan; then Manmatha intervenes and tells her not to go as he, with the help of his arrows, will make Shiva surrender to her; in a sneering tone Parvati tells Manmatha that he is no match for Shiva; by worshipping Shiva, she will make him marry her; Parvati's close friends also warn Manmatha not to attack Shiva; but, turning a deaf ear to them he attacks; Shiva opens his third eye and Manmatha turns into ashes while uttering Mother! Oh Mother! Then Rati Devi – wife of Manmatha- pleads with Shiva to revive her husband. Parvati also appeals to Shiva to make Manmatha alive. Shiva relents, revives Manmatha and marries Parvati. Salutations to Shiva, Parvati and Kuchipudi Venugopala.

Commentary: This Yakshgana was written by the scholar poet Malladi Ramakrishna Sastry. The singer composer Ghantasala used a number of ragas comprising the 'Raga-Tala-Malika'. The ragas used by the singer-composer were: 'Hamsaanandi, Naata, Shankarabharanam, Anandabairavi, Nata, Madhyamavati, Kambhoji, Atana-Misrachapu, Kedaragoula, Shahana, Saraswati, Hindola, Saavari, Aarabhi, Sriraga-Kandachapu'. The 'Aarti' in Ghantasala's voice while rendering this Yakshgana was so appealing that the Periya Swami Chandra Sekhara Yatiraja specially invited Ghantasala to sing it in his Kanchi Ashram premises.

Notes

1. The commentaries on "Pushpavilapam' and "Kuntikumari' are based on K. Rohini Prasad's interpretation
2. The rest of the commentaries are based on M. Purushottamacharya' book, Mana Ghantasala SangeetaVaibhavam

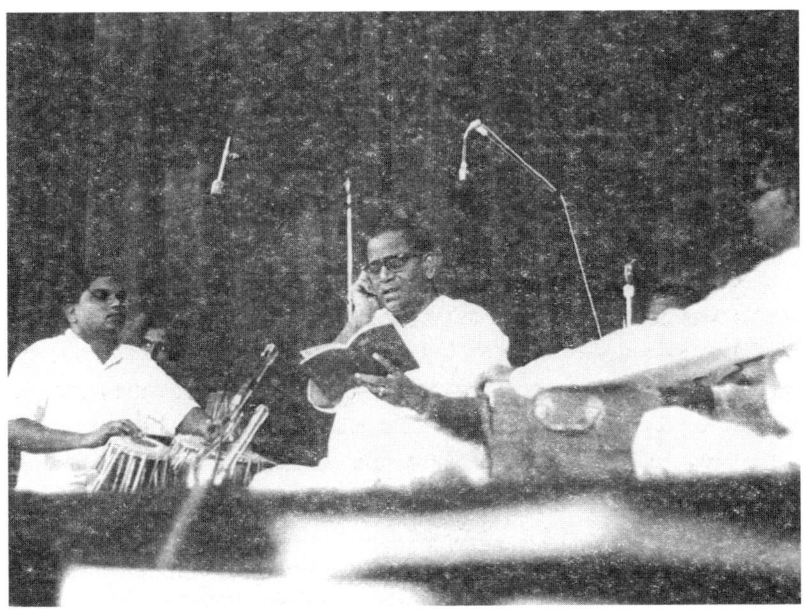

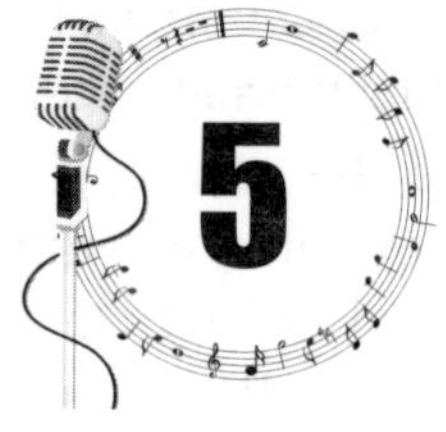

The Era of Ghantasala

(a): Contemporary Lyricists, Music Composers and Singers

In India, we believe in the concept of *'Swarna Yug'* (Golden Era). In Indian history, we call the Gupta period, a Swarna Yug. It was perhaps due to some divine plan that all those blessed with great acumen, be it literature, music or acting came together during the particular period and made it a 'Golden Era'. Lyricists with lofty ideas like (Senior) Samudrala Raghavacharyulu, Malladi Ramakrishna Shastry, Pingali, Devulapalli Krishna Shastry, Sri Sri, Arudra, Atreya, Dasaradhi, Kosaraju, (Junior) Samudrala and C. Narayana Reddy adorned the firmament of Telugu film world. Astounding composers like C. R. Subburaman, S. Rajeswararao, Ghantasala, Pendyala, Susarla Dakshinamurthy, Venu, T. V. Raju, M. S. Vishwanathan - Rammurthy, K. V. Mahadevan and T. Chalapathi Rao were ruling the roost; melodious male singers like Ghantasala, P. B. Srinivos,

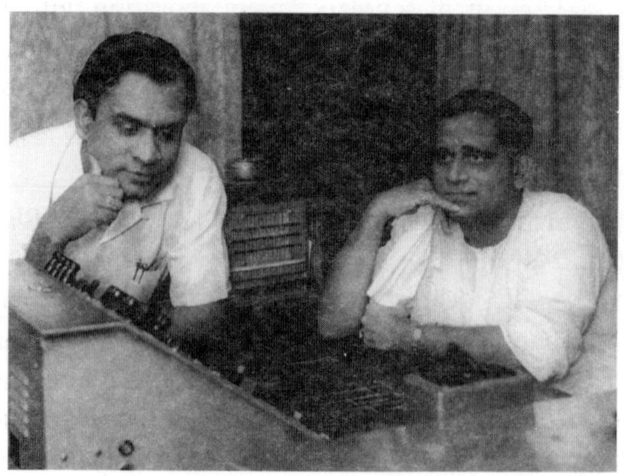

Madavapeddi, A. M. Raja and Pitapuram and sonorous female singers like Balasaraswati, P. Bhanumathi, P. Susheela, P. Leela, Jikki, and S. Janaki were enthralling the audiences.[1]

Moreover, the roles of the lyricist, the music composer and the singer are equally important in creating a musical piece. They should work in tandem and should have cordial and complete understanding with each other. With that regard, Ghantasala had perfect understanding with the lyrists, music composers and co singers he worked with.

LYRICISTS

1. (Senior) Samudrala Raghavacharyulu

Senior Samudrala was a family friend of Savitri Ghantasala. Having listened to the melodious voice of Ghantasala, Samudrala wanted him to go to Madras for exploring opportunities in the movie world. Having got substantial influence in film industry, Samudrala introduced Ghantasala to the reckonable people, made him do *'Kacheris'* and got him a position in All India Radio. In a nutshell, Samudrala was the benefactor of Ghantasala. Ghantasala - Samudrala combination produced the enticing and soulful songs in *"Devadas"*, *"Bhukailas"*, *"Suvarnasundari"*, *"Tenali Ramakrishna"* *"Pandavavanavasam"* *"Lava Kusa"* and *"Sarangadhara"*.

2. Malladi Ramakrishna Shastri

He was a highly learned man who learnt the Vedas and the Brahma sutras from great scholars. In collaboration with Malladi, Ghantasala came out with memorable songs in movies like *"Jayabheri"* *"Chiranjeevulu"*. These songs were praised by even classical musicians like Nedunuri Krishnamoorty.

3. Pingali

Vijaya productions produced classics like *"Paatala Bhairavi"*, *"Pellichesichudu"*, *"Mayabazaar"*, *"Jagadekaveeruni Katha"*, *"Appu Chesi Pappu Koodu"*, "Gundamma Katha" which had memorable songs sung by Ghantasala. Can you believe that all those meaningful songs were written by Pingali the great? Pingali wrote songs for other movies like *"Mahamantri Timmarusu"*, *"Satya Harischandra"* *"Sri Krishnarjuna Yuddham" and "Prameelarjuneeyam"*.

4. Devulapalli Krishna Shastry

He was called Andhra Shelley. Sastry's poetry was romantic and passionate which was appropriate for fine arts like music and dance. He came to limelight in the Telugu movie world thanks to the lyrics and story he wrote for *"Malleshwari"*. He penned more than 150 lyrics for 70 movies like *"Malleshwari", "Bangaru Papa", "Rajamakutam", "Bangaru Panjaram", "Undamma Bottu Pedtha"* and *"Ekaveera"*. Ghantasala – Devulapalli combination produced enthralling songs in classics like *"Malleswari", "Kalasina Manasulu"*, and *"Sipayi Chinnayya"*.

5. Sri Sri

He was the first modern Telugu poet to write about the common man and contemporary issues. His *magnum opus* was *"Mahaprasthanam"*. Ghantasala - Sri Sri combination has given some of the best inspiring, patriotic, revolutionary and romantic songs like *"Paadavoyi Bharateeyuda", "Kalakanidi", "Teluguveeralevara", "Evarivo Neevarivo", "Manasuna Manasai" and "Payaninchemanavalapula"*. It surprises everybody to know that an atheist like Sri Sri penned the famous *'Harikatha' "Srinagaja Thanayam"* in the movie *"Vagdanam"*.

6. Arudra

Arudra was a scholar poet. His *magnum opus* was *"Samagra Andhra Saahityam"*. He had close friendship with Ghantasala. Ghantasala - Arudra combination made possible memorable romantic songs like *"Oohalu Gusa Gusa Lade", "Eee Musi Musi Navvula Virisina", "Evaru Leni Chota" and "Yamuna Teeramuna", "Neeli Meghalalo" and " Rambha Urvasi Taladanne"*

7. Aatreya

Can you think of movies like *"Atmabalam", "Moogamanasulu", "Manchi Manasulu" "Muralikrishna" "Daagudumuthalu," "Premnagar", "Sumangali", "Sri Venkateshwara Mahatmyam" and "Dr. Chakravarti"* etc without the memorable songs produced by Ghantasala - Atreya combination?

8. Dasaradhi

He was a revolutionary poet whose major work was *"Timiramamtho Samaram"* (fight with darkness). The down-trodden, poor and exploited workers were his subjects in poetry.

Ghantasala - Dasaradhi combination was responsible for some of the best *'Bhakti'* (devotional) songs of Telugu movies. *"Nadireyi E Jaamulo", "Jagadabhirama Raghukulasoma", "Jayahe Nava Neela Megha Shyama", "Veyi Venuvula Mroge Vela"* and for some romantic songs in movies like *"Vasantasena."*

9. Kosaraju

Humorous songs in Telugu movies were mainly contributed by Kosaraju. Some of the movies are *"Bharyabharthalu", "Bhalerangadu", "Manchimanasuku Manchirojulu", "Atmeeyulu", "Namminabantu", "Rojulumaarayi" and "Poolarangadu".*

10. (Junior) Samudrala

He wrote some of the fine songs sung by Ghantasala: *"Andame Aanandam", "Hara Hara Sambho", "Virisindi Vinta Haayi", "Vannela Chinnela Nera", "Raave Naacheliya", "Raave Radharaniraave", "Raagaala Saragala"* and *"Puvai Virisina Punnami Vela".*

11. C. Narayana Reddy

He is also a scholar-poet. He is well known for his critical works like *"Aadhunikaandhra Kavitvamu"*. Ghantasala – C. Narayana Reddy combination produced marvelous romantic songs: *"Nannudochu Konduvate", "Kila Kila Navvulu Chilikina", Kannuleevela Chilipiga Navvenu", "Chamanti Enduke Ee Vinta", Kanulu Kanulu Kalisenu", "Anta Kopamaite Nenenta Badhapadatano", "Antaga Nanu Chudaku", "Thotalo Naa Raju". "Bhale Manchi Roju"* was one of the best songs sung by Ghantasala in 1970's.

MUSIC COMPOSERS

Music composers and singers should have harmonious relations with each other. If there is a discord between the music composer and the singer, the harmony of the song will be adversely affected. Ghantasala, by nature was a humble and polite person; he never quarreled with his colleagues. So, his relations with the music composers he worked with were smooth and cordial.

1. C. R. Subburaman

He was known as a genius in film music. Music composers like S. Rajeswara Rao, Ghantasala, Susarla Dakshinamurthy, M. S. Vishwanathan – Ramamurthy- who later became famous – started their careers as co-music directors of Subburaman. Even though he died at the age of 28, he composed music for 41 movies in Telugu and Tamil. Ghantasala was his co-music director for the movies entitled *"Ratnamala"* and *"Balaraju"*. Ghantasala melodiously sang for the movies for which music was composed by Subburaman – his magnum opus being "Devadas". In one way, Subburaman was Ghantasala's mentor. R.Balasaraswati Devi said that Subburaman admired the music composed by Ghantasala for the movie *"Shavukaru"*.[2]

2. S. Rajeswara rao

He was a child prodigy who gave stage performances at the age of seven. He was a pioneer in the field of light music (*'Lalita Sangeetam'*) and his records and his songs over All India Radio became very popular. Like Ghantasala, he was also associated with Vijayanagaram Maharaja Music College and Dwaram Venkataswami Naidu. When he was in Calcutta, he was closely associated with K. L. Saigal and Pankaj Mullick and learnt Hindustani music. He could play a number of musical instruments. He composed music for more than 100 movies in Telugu and Tamil. His favorite classical five ragas are like his *'Pancha pranaas'* (Five pranas): *'Bheempalaas', 'Sindhubhairavi', 'Kapi', 'Kalyani'* and *'Pahaadi'*. [3] Ghantasala had friendly relations with S. Rajeshwara Rao and in fact at family level too, they had cordial relations. In most of the Telugu movies for which S. Rajeshwara Rao composed music, Ghantasala sang melodious songs. *"Malleeswari", "Bhale Ramudu", "Charanadaasi", "Bhale Ammayilu", "Chenchu Lakshmi", "Appu Chesi Pappu Kudu", "Rani Ratnaprabha", "Bhakta Jayadeva", "Iddaru Mitrulu", "Bharyabhartalu", "Aradhana", "Bhishma", "Kulagotralu", "Chaduvukunna Ammayilu", "Amara Shilpi Jakkanna", "Bobbili Yuddham" and "Dr. Chakravarti."*

"I like Ghantasala and P. Leela among singers", declared S. Rajeswara Rao.[4]

3. Susarla Dakshinamurthy

He belonged to a family of musicians and sang a few songs for the movies too. He composed music for more than 135 movies in Telugu, Tamil, Kannada and Sinhalese. Being an expert in classical music, Ghantasala had close relationship with Susarla. This great composer made Lata Mangeshkar sing *"Nidura Pora Tammuda"* in the movie "*Santhanam*" with impeccable Telugu pronunciation. The sequel song was sung by Ghantasala. Some of Susarla's prominent movies for which Ghantasala sang were: *"Samsaram", "Santhanam", "Annapurna", "Nartanasala" and "Harishchandra".* The *'padyams'* rendered in the movies *"Nartanasala" and "Harischandra" received* critical acclaim and would tell the cognoscenti the respective idiolects used by Ghantasala for singing differently for NTR and SVR. It tells about the singer as well as the music director.

4. Pendyala

Pendyala was one of the most successful music composers of the Southern Indian film field. His favorite ragas are: *'Bheempalas', 'Peelu', 'Kalyani', 'Sindhubhairavi', 'Reetigoula', 'Jayajayawanti', 'Malkauns', 'Darbari Kanada'* and 'Vatdeep'.[5] He composed music for about 70 movies. Among the prominent movies for which Pendyala composed music, Ghantasala sang melodious and memorable songs for the following; *"Drohi", "Kannatalli", "Dongaramudu" "Bavamaradallu", "Jayabheri", "Sri Venkateshwara Mahatmyam", "Mahamantri Thimmarusu", "Mahakavi Kalidas", "Ramudu - Bhimudu", "Vagdanam", "MLA", "Bhattivikramarka", "Jagadekaveeruni Katha", "Sri Krishnarjunayuddham", "Bandipotudongalu" and "Sri Krishnatulabharam".*

5. Adinarayana Rao

VAK Rangarao declared: *"Adinarayana Rao is credited for introducing Hindustani music in contemporary flavor and simplified orchestration, and thereby impressing both laymen audience as well cognoscenti. It is this music that survives him which enthralls all the music lovers".*

Adinarayana Rao too like Ghantasala, was a product of Maharaja Music College, Vijayanagaram. He produced 15 movies in Telugu, Tamil and Hindi and composed music for about 25 movies. Memorable compositions from him are: *"Rajasekhara Neepai Moju Teera Ledura", "Hayi Hayi Ga Aamani Saage" "Ghana Ghana Sundara" and "Telugu Veera Levara".* Ghantasala sang mesmerizing songs in most of the movies for which Adinarayana Rao composed music.

6. Master Venu

His passion for music took him to Vasant Desai and Naushad Ali. It made an indelible impact on his compositions.[6] Master Venu contributed to the re-recording of *"Paatala Bhairavi"*, *"Shavukaru"*, *"Chandraharam", and "Pelli Chesichudu"* for which Ghantasala was the music director. One can imagine the friendly relations between Ghantasala and Master Venu. Ghantasala sang sonorous songs for the movies for which Master Venu was the music director. Those are *"Rojulu Maaraayi"*, *"Peddarikalu"*, *"Todikodallu"*, *"Mangalya Balam"*, *"Nammina Bantu"*, *"Rajamakutam"*, *"Kalasi Unte Kaladu Sukam"*, *"Pellikani Pillalu"*, *"Siri Sampadalu"*, *"Murali Krishna"*, *"Adugujadalu" and "Naadi Adajanme"*.

7. Viswanathan - Ramamoorthy

They were a southern Indian music composer duo comprising M. S. Vishwanathan - T. K. Ramamoorthy. The duo had worked together since 1952 for over 100 movies till the split came in 1965. Both of them acknowledge C. R. Subburaman as their mentor. M. S. Viswanathan composed the tune and music for Ghantasala's famous song *"Jagamemaya"* and its Tamil version. Ghantasala sang enticing songs for some of the movies for which music was composed by M. S. Vishwanathan. These are: *"Tenali Ramakrishna"*, *"Kutumba Gauravam"*, *"Manchi Chedu"*.

8. T. V. Raju

To start with T. V. Raju worked as an assistant to the music composer Adinarayana Rao. It seems N. T. Rama Rao, S. V. Ranga Rao and T. V. Raju lived in the same house in their initial days in Madras.[7] Keeping in view their friendship, N. T. Rama Rao made him work for his own production NAT Films as music director. He composed music for 35 movies. Some of the movies for which T. V. Raju composed memorable music are: *"Pichchi Pullaiah"*, *"Jayasimha"*, *"Chintamani"*, *"Panduranga Mahatmyam"*, *"Sati Sulochana"*, *"Balanagamma"*, *"Sri Krishna Pandaveeyam"*, *"Sri Krishnaavataram"*, *"Ummadi Kutumbam"*, *"Saptaswaralu"*, and *"Sri Krishnanjaneya Yuddham"*.

9. K. V. Mahadevan

Among the music composers of the Southern India, Mahadevan had the largest career, spanning about 6 decades. He became a popular music composer in Telugu film field: highly respected directors like Bapu and K. Vishwanath insisted on having him as the music director for their movies. Some of the memorable songs composed by Mahadevan were sung by Ghantasala in movies like *"Manchimansulu"*, *"Moogamansulu"*, *"Anthastulu"*, *"Asthiparulu"*, *"Sampoorna Ramayanam"* and *"Badipanthulu"*. In the post Ghantasala period, Mahadevan composed music for movies like *"Shankarabharam"*, *"Swatimutyam"*, *"Sagarasangamam"*, *"Sirivennela"*, *"Saptapadi"*, *"Vamsha Vriksham"* and *"Swati Kiranam"*.

10. Ashwatthama

He was also associated with Maharaja Music College of Vijayanagaram and Dwaram Venkataswamy Naidu. Even when he was a budding music composer, his tunes were appreciated by stalwarts like D. K. Pattammal and Radha Jayalakshmi.[8] Ghantasala sang for movies like *"Maa Inti Mahalakshmi"*, *"Anna Tammudu"*, *"Sri Krishnarayabaram"* and *"Mayani Mamata"*.

11. T. Chalapati Rao

He composed music for about 50 movies in Telugu, Tamil and Kannada. He created many popular songs for films starring Akkineni Nageswara Rao. As Ghantasala was the voice of Akkineni in those days, he sang sonorously for the movies for which Chalapati Rao composed music. According to Chalapati Rao, Ghantasala would do *'Parakayapravesham'* i.e. he gets into the body of the actor – it could be Akkineni, N. T. Ramarao or even Relangi and creates, through his song, the necessary emotion or mood for heightening the aesthetics of the situation. For example, if Ghantasala sings for Akkineni, he makes *'Laalitya'* (mellifluousness) manifest in *"Bhakta Jayadeva"*; supposing Ghantasala sings for NTR, he makes *'Gaambhirya'* (seriousness) manifest in *"Sri Sitaramakalyanam"*; and by chance, if Ghantasala sings for Relangi, he makes the *'haasya'* (humour) manifest in *'Mayabazaar'*.[9]

12. P. Sangeeta Rao

He is the eldest son of Ghantasala's guru, Patrayani Sitarama Shastry. He was also an assistant director to Ghantasala. He says that Ghantasala became a trend setter for the entire Southern India in rendering songs in a particular way. He added that Ghantasala had love and respect not only for the classical music but also for *'Desi'* music comprising a variety of folk songs.[10]

13. J. V. Raghavulu

He was an assistant director to Ghantasala for decades. He composed music for about 50 movies out of which *"Jeevanatarangalu"* was well known. Ghantasala sang meaningful songs for this movie. He said that 'Light music concerts' (lalitha sangeeta kacheris) started with Ghantasala. He was all praise for the humble, polite and friendly nature of Ghantasala.

14. Vijaya Krishna Murthy

He was an assistant director to Ghantasala in Vijaya productions. In movies like *"Gulebakavali Katha"*- for which Vijaya Krishnamurthy was the music director along with Joseph-Ghantasala sang memorable songs like *"Nannu Dochu Konduvate"*. He also composed music for *"Aggidora"* *"Aggiveerudu"* and *"Rajakota Rahasyam"*. Krishnamurthy was all praise for Ghantasala's greatness.

15. Pandit Janardan Mitta:

He is a maestro of the Sitar and a disciple of Pandit Ravi Shankar. He has been in Madras film industry since 1959. As a close associate of Ghantasala, he played the Sitar for several movies for which Ghantasala composed music and accompanied the singer-composer on his trips abroad. He composed some of the private songs of Ghantasala for which C. Narayana Reddy was the lyricist.

CO-SINGERS

Encomiums are conferred on and eulogies are written about people who hold high positions or who wield a lot of power or pelf. But the ultimate and extremely valuable tribute is that which is paid by one's colleagues and competitors.

1. P. Bhanumati

She was known for her versatility. She was a multilingual actress, singer, writer, music director, director and producer. She acted in over 200 films in Telugu and Tamil. She sang beautiful duets with Ghantasala for *"Malleeswari"* which would not be forgotten by the music lovers: *"Aakasa Veedhilo haayiga Egirevu"*, *"Parugulu Teeyali"* or *"Ouna nija mena"*. Talking about Ghantasala

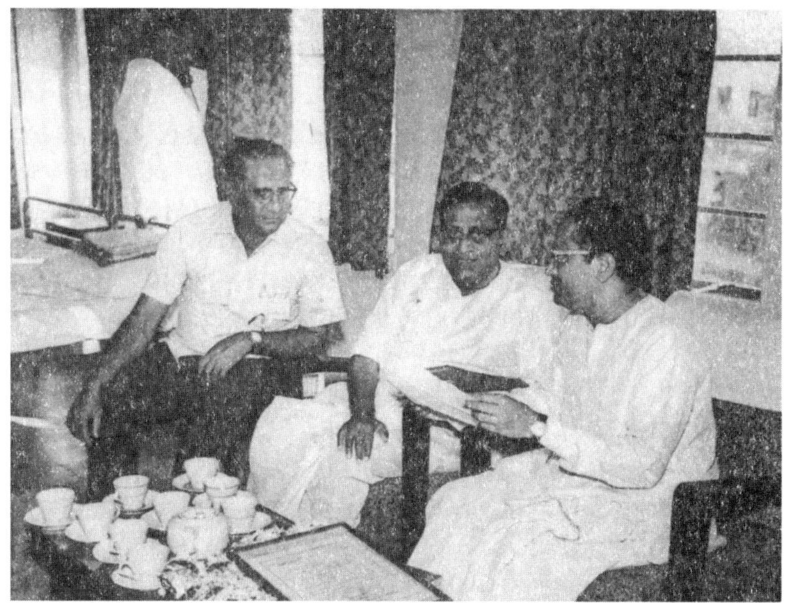

she said that he was the only male singer who could compete with her in singing. It seems Ghantasala also thought that to sing with Bhanumati was a challenge.[11] In her tribute paid to Ghantasala, Bhanumati said that the great male singer wanted every song of his to be distinct and that she thought that he should have sang for her movie *"Vipranarayana"* too. She and her husband were family friends of Ghantasala.

2. R. Balasaraswati Devi

She was a child prodigy. At the age of six, her voice was recorded for the first solo gramophone record by HMV. Her forte are sad songs and lullabies, memorable among them are *"Bangaru Papayi Bahumathulu Pondali"* and *"Dharaniki Giri Bharama"* She sang for all the great music composers of her time: Nagaiah, Subburaman, Ghantasala, S. Dakshinamurthy, B. Rajanikanta rao, T. V. Raju, Master Venu and even Naushad. She sang memorable duets mostly with Ghantasala namely *"Madiloni Madhura Bhavana"* and *"Ella velalandu nee Chakkani Chirunavvulakai"*.

3. P. Leela

She was a Malayalee with a sound background in carnatic music. Ghantasala introduced her to Telugu film field. With veneration for Ghantasala, Leela stated in 'Mee Ghantasala': *"He explained the meaning of and the emotion necessary for the songs, the intonation (including the stress) part of it and made me do rehearsals at least for 4 times. Singing for "LavaKusa" for which music was composed by Ghantasala- was a milestone in my life. He made me sing so well that none would believe that my mother tongue wasn't Telugu, the credit goes to Ghantasala. He gave invaluable suggestions to his colleagues. We can't come across such a person again".*[12] P. Leela sang memorable duets with Ghantasala in a number of movies. Prominent among them *are "Patala Bhairavi", "Jaysimha", "Chiranjeevulu", "Mayabazaar", "Babruvahana", "Appuchesi Pappu Kuudu", "RajaMakutam"* and *"Sri Panduranga Mahatmyam".*

4. Jikki

Her original name was P. G. Krishnaveni. She married the playback singer A. M. Rajah. She sang sonorously in about 100 Telugu movies and 70 Tamil movies; she sang in Kannada, Malayalam and Simhalese too. Keeping in view her peculiar, impressive and enticing voice, and range of singing, we can call her the Geeta Dutt of Southern Indian Film world. She had immense respect for Ghantasala. In the book, Mee Ghantasala, Jikki wrote, *"Ghantasala- as a music composer- knew which song should be given to which singer and he had the skill to extract the best out of the singer. I was fortunate to have sung melodious duets with him in movies like "Anaarkali" "Suvarna Sundari", "Chenchulakshmi", "Donga Ramudu", "Rojulu Maraayi", and "Shantinivasam". Ghantasala's 'Gaatramaadhuryam' (melodious singing) will never be forgotten by people. He was demigod for film world".*[13]

5. Madavapeddi Satyam

Like Ghantasala he was also born in 1922. He sang his first Telugu song in film industry along with Ghantasala for the movie *"Laila Majnu" (*1949). In rendering Telugu Padyam, he was comparable to Ghantasala. He sang many songs and *'padyams'* for the movies for which Ghantasala composed music. In 1981, he told the author (i.e. me) that unlike in the contemporary cinema world, Ghantasala gave him and PBS a number of opportunities to sing.[14] His famous songs are *"Vivahabhojanambu", "Bhali Bhali Bhali Deva"* and *"Thadhimi Thakadhimi".* When Ghantasala was the voice of Akkineni and NTR, Madhavapeddi was the voice of S. V. Ranga Rao. He sang humorous songs for Relangi and Ramana Reddy as well.

6. P. B. Srinivos

Famous playback singer P. B. Srinivos - who was younger to Ghantasala by 8 years, sang melodiously in Telugu, Tamil, Kannada and Malayalam. In his book entitled 'Swaralahari' PBS allotted a full chapter to Ghantasala wherein he vividly described the various abilities of Ghantasala as singer and music director. In a poetic tribute paid to Ghantasala, PBS calls his senior and mentor *'Chitraranga Parthasaradhi'*. (Lord Parthasaradhi in the Kurukshetra of the film world).[15] Keeping in view the young PBS's future in the film field, his maternal uncle gave him the records of Ghantasala of that period. In perhaps one of his last interviews, he told the author (i.e. me) that he practiced Ghantasala's *'padyams'* from *"Pushpavilapam"* and *"Kuntikumari"* and also other popular songs of Ghantasala of that period. He added that he and his mother would shed tears as they remained moved by the pathos that Ghantasala could evoke. In the later years, Ghantasala became his mentor, his co-singer and his competitor in the southern India film field. Ghantasala predicted a bright future for PBS who was just a budding singer then. PBS told me that Ghantasala used to affectionately call him *'Tammudu'* (younger brother in Telugu). Ghantasala appreciated the way PBS sang *"O Ho Gulabi Bala"* for the movie *"Manchi Manishi"*; also PBS melodiously sang *"Nilave Ennidam Nerungathe"* for the Tamil movie *"Ramu"* which was composed by Pendyala. During this interview, PBS recalled how Ghantasala was demigod for Pendyala. When Pendyala asked Ghantasala to sing the Telugu version of the song, Ghantasala apparently remarked *"Tammudu has sung it so beautifully in Tamil. With my poor health can I sing it as beautifully as he did?"*[16] In the movies for which Ghantasala composed music, he made PBS sing beautiful duets with P. Susheela in *"Gudigantalu"*, *"Rakta Sambhandham"* and *"Shanti Nivasam"*.

7. P. Susheela

Like Ghantasala, Susheela was also a product of the famous Maharaja college of Music, Vijayanagaram. She sang thousands of duets with Ghantasala which became exceedingly popular. In a tribute paid to Ghantasala, Susheela said that the beauty of his voice did not change at all the three 'Sthayees' (levels) – *'Mandra Sthayee'*, *'Madhyama Sthayee'*, and *'Taraa Sthayee'*, that his voice gave life to all the *'Nava Rasas'* (Nine rasas) and that he made use of

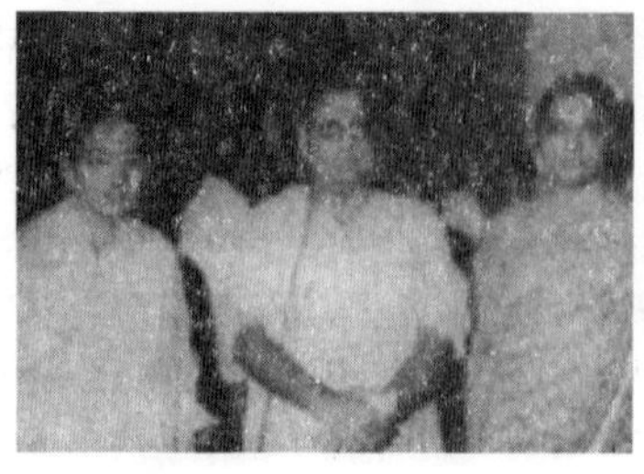

not only classical music but also folk music, *'Harikatha'*, *'Burrakatha'*, *'Yakshagana'* and *'Bhavageet'*.[17] She recorded thousands of songs in several Indian languages: Telugu, Tamil, Kannada, Malayalam, Hindi, Bengali, Oriya, Sanskrit and Tulu. She has been recognized by both the Guinness book of world records and the Asian Book of records. A conservative estimate of her total number of songs puts it between 25,000 and 30,000.

8. Pithapuram Nageswara Rao

He mostly contributed humorous songs to Telugu movies. Ghantasala gave him opportunities to sing in the movies for which he composed music. He sang along with Madhavapeddi. Some of the popular humorous songs like *"Ayyayyo Jebulo Dabbulu Poyene"*, *"Chepite Vintiva Guruguru"*, *"Evaru Chesina Karma"*, *"Buddhochchena Neeku Manasa"*, *"Parama Gurudu Cheppina Vaadu Peddamanishi"*, and *"Raavela Dayaleda Raava Intiki Baala"*.

9. S. Janaki

She has sung in 15 Indian and foreign languages. She is a reckonable singer in Telugu, Tamil, Kannada and Malayalam. While discussing Ghantasala's greatness, Janaki averred *"He gave us very useful suggestions; some singers have done music composing; but they are not successful as composers. He was unique. He lives forever in our hearts. He has attained immortality"*. Janaki sang a number of duets with Ghantasala and PBS. Her memorable devotional duet with Ghantasala is *"Nadireyi E Jamulo Swami"*.[18]

10. S. P. Balasubramaniam (Balu)

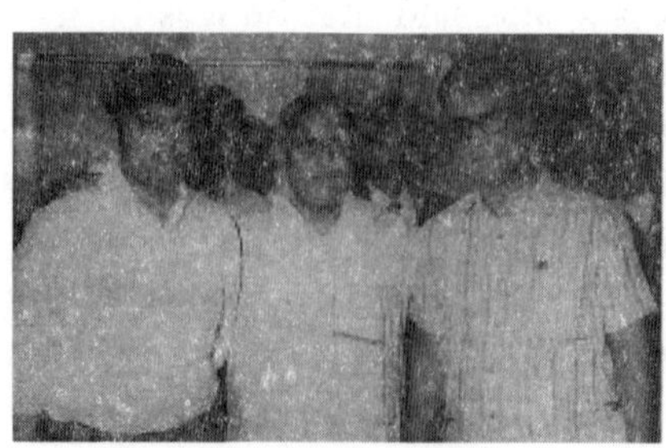

When Balasubramaniam was a budding singer in the late 1960's and early 1970's, Ghantasala encouraged him by appreciating the young singer's talents and by recommending him to the music composers to sing songs like *"Charana*

Kinkinulu Ghallu Ghallu Mana" in lieu of him. Balu has followed Ghantasala's style of singing songs and of rendering *'padyams'* and *'stotras'*. By following the path laid by Ghantasala, Balu has become a successful singer and a successor to Ghantasala in terms of popularity. In the book entitled 'Mee Ghantasala', Balu wrote in a poetic manner *"Ghantasala is the surname of a Gandharva; without listening to the songs sung by Ghantasala, not only ordinary human beings, but also the gods do not wake up"*.[19] Balu's popular song sung with Ghantasala is *"Pratiraatri Vasantaraatri"* in the movie *"Ekaveera"*.

NON TELUGU SINGERS

11. T. M. Sounderarajan

He was popularly known as TMS. Even though he was the reigning king in Tamil field industry for more than four decades, TMS was a great fan of Ghantasala. In the initial days Ghantasala recommended TMS to some Tamil music composers and producers. TMS sang songs composed by Ghantasala and admitted that he could not sing songs like *"Shiva Shankari"*. [20]

12. Lata Mangeshkar

She is one of the greatest singers of India. The singing career spanned over seven decades. One of her gurus was Aman Ali Khan; he was fond of carnatic music.[21] Her father, Deenanath Mangeshkar - who was a classical singer and a theatre artist- sang *'Tygaraja Kritis'* which came in record form. Lataji's association with and admiration for Ghantasala started from the days of her recording of the famous Telugu song *"Nidura Pora Thammuda"*. She sang it mellifluously for the movie *"Santhanam"* for which the music composer was S. Dakshina Murthy. After listening to the sequel song sung by Ghantasala, she said that he was blessed with a marvelous voice and he sang it in the right mood. Later she advised him not to take water or food given by others as the world abounded with jealous people.[22] Alas! Ghantasala followed the advice given by Lataji! In an interview given to the The Hindu newspaper sometime in 2009, Lataji said even though she had listened to many renditions of The Bhagavat Gita, she thought Ghantasala's was excellent.[23]

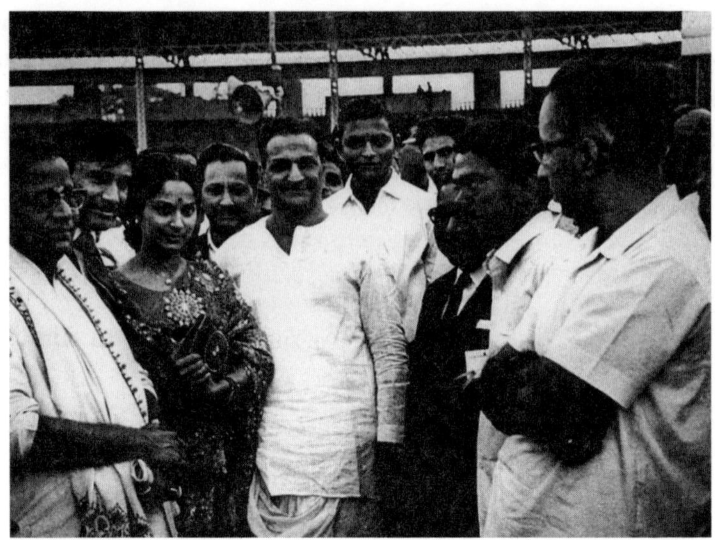

13. Mohd. Rafi

He was one of the most popular singers of the Hindi film field. He was known for his versatility and his songs ranged from classical numbers to patriotic songs, Qawaalis to Ghazals. Two songs sung by Ghantasala in Telugu were later sung by Rafi in Hindi: *"Hayi Hayi Ga Aamani Saage"* (Telugu) versus *"Kuhu Kuhu Bhole Koyaliya"* (Hindi); *"Payaninche O Chiluka"* (Telugu) versus *"Chal Udja Re Panchi"* (Hindi). Rafi was magnanimous enough to admit that Ghantasala sang those songs in a better manner than him. Also, Rafi was fond of Ghantasala's *"Shiva Shankari"*.[24]

14. K. J. Yesudas

He is one of the most accomplished singers in India. Like Ghantasala; he is also a classically trained playback singer. He regularly performs kacheries in carnatic music. His music career has spanned five decades. He has exceedingly admired Ghantasala's songs. Moreover, his admiration for the senior singer made him unveil the statue of Ghantasala in Guntur, Andhra Pradesh.

Generally speaking, senior singers - who wield a lot of influence and power-, would not allow the other singers to come up. This is applicable to the Southern Indian as well as Hindi film field. On he contrary, Ghantasala was magnanimous in his approach. In he movies for which he composed music he gave suitable songs to Madhavapeddi, P. B. Srinivos and Pithapuram. He encouraged female singers like A. P. Komala, Swarnalatha, Jamuna Rani, Vaidehi and K. Rani by giving them tunes suitable to them. He recommended younger singers like S. P. Balasubramanyam and V. Ramakrishna to his fellow music composers; he made S. P. Balasubramanyam sing for the movie *"Tulasi"* for which he conducted music.

Notes

1. During the same period 'Swarna Yug' took place in Hindi film field.
2. Smruti Tarangalu, *p*. 40
3. Swaralahari, *p*. 16
4. Mee Ghantasala, *p*. 70
5. Swaralahari, *p*. 64
6. Ibid, *p*. 28
7. Ibid, *p*. 87
8. Ibid, *p*. 80
9. Mee Ghantasala, *p*. 83
10. Ibid, *p*. 113
11. Ibid,
12. Ibid, *p*. 49
13. Ibid, *p*. 52
14. When the auhor met Madhava *p*eddi in 1981, he expressed his opinion
15. Mee Ghantasala, *p*. 115
16. In an interview given to the author, P. B. S told him so
17. Mee Ghantasala, *p*. 51
18. Ibid, *p*. 53
19. Ibid, *p*. 46
20. Ghantasala Jnapakalu, *p*. 104
21. Kodavatiganti Rohini *p*rasad, Sangeetham; Reethulu Lotulu; Hyderabad 2014, *p*. 124
22. Ghantasala Jnapakalu, *p*. 122–123
23. Ibid, *p*. 110
24. Ibid, *p*. 104; *p*. 210

(b): Contemporary Actors, Directors and Producers

Demeanor plays a vital role in human relations - more so in the movie world. Ghantasala was, by nature, humble, polite and tolerant person. He tolerated the idiosyncrasies and tantrums of directors and producers. Though both goddess Saraswati and goddess Lakshmi had showered their blessings on Ghantasala, his success did not go to his head. As a result, he had smooth relations with actors, directors and producers.

ACTORS

1. Akkenini Nageswara Rao

He was popularly known as ANR. Out of the 250 movies in which ANR acted, Ghantasala sang for him in 200 movies. When Ghantasala passed away, ANR said that he lost his voice and that he owed half of his success to Ghantasala. In the book Mee Ghantasala, ANR averred; *"In his songs Ghantasala used to manifest through his voice the emotions or mood required for the situation and did half of the work to be done by the actor. This made the work of the actor easy. Some live even after their death. Ghantasala is one of them. He will, forever live in our hearts. We started our careers in the film field during the same period. He was a pillar of strength to me and contributed to my progress".*[1]

2. Nandamuri Taraka Rama Rao

He was popularly known as NTR. From 1950 to 1974, Ghantasala sang for NTR in 99% of the movies in which NTR played roles. It could be a social movie like *"Shavukaru"* or a mythological movie like *"Sri Krishnatulabharam"* or it could be a historical period movie dealing with kings like *"Mahamantri Timmarusu"*, Ghantasala was NTR's voice and he came out with appropriate *'Rasa'* (emotion or mood) in rendering duets and solos, *'padyams'* and *'stotras'*. NTR wrote about Ghantasala "With his incomparable voice, he entertained millions of people and he was not only Andhra's pride but also the pride of entire India. He not only served the nation by melodious music, but also by being in the forefront for serving the society - during Chinese aggression, war with Pakistan, cyclone relief program or Police Welfare Fund."[2]

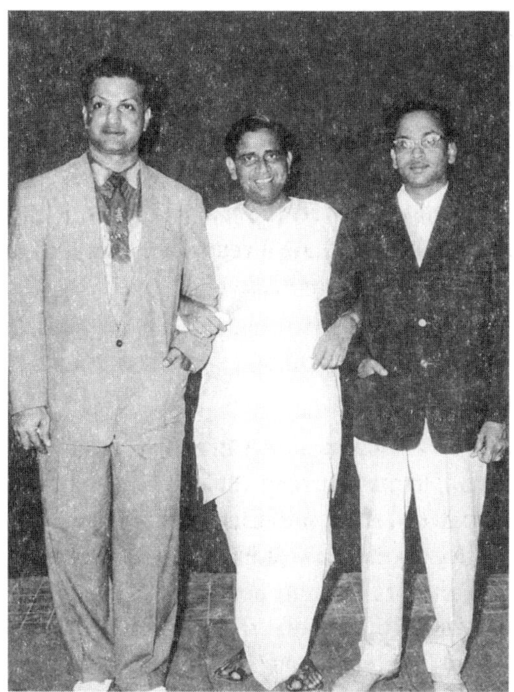

3. Relangi Venkataramaiah

He was popularly known as Relangi. He was one of the finest comedians known for his comic expressions and dialogues. He acted in hundreds of Telugu movies. He sang for himself in movies like *"Missamma"*. Ghantasala sang memorable songs for him in movies like *"Mayabazaar"*, *"Apucheesi Pappu Kudu"* and *"Vagdanam"*. The songs were *"Sundari Neevanti Divya Swaroopamu"*, *"Kaasiki Poyanu Rama Hari"* and *"Sri Nagaja Tanayam"*. The stalwart singer, it appears, got into the body of Relangi; *'Parakaya pravesam'* [3] and sang with the right amount of nuances of humor, comic expressions and accent. In some of the movies like *"Keelugurram"* and *"Patala Bhairavi"*, Ghantasala made Relangi sing for himself.

4. S. V. Ranga Rao

He was popularly known as SVR. He was known for his versatility, histrionic talent and mesmerizing dialogues. Ghantasala sang a series of profound *'padyams'* like *"Mayameya Jagamme Nityamani"* in *"Harishchandra"* (1956) which were pictured on

SVR. *"Dhanamera Annitiki Moolam"* was one of the best songs sung by Ghantasala for SVR.

5. Gummadi Venkateswara Rao

He was popularly known as Gummadi. He was known for his histrionic talent. He did justice to every role given to him, for example *"Mahamantri Timmarusu"*. He had high regard for Ghantasala who sung for him the immortal song *"Dinakara Shubhakara"* in the movie *"Vinayaka Chavithi"*. In the interviews, Gummadi reiterated that he had high regard for two persons in the film field – One is Chittoor Nagaiah and the second, Ghantasala.[4]

6. T. L. Kanta Rao

In historical period movies- esp. of the producer Vithalacharya – Kanta Rao shone like a real prince. In mythological movies he was next only to NT Rama Rao. For example, in the movie *"Lava Kusa"*, no one else could play the role of Lakshman as effectively as Kanta Rao. In the classic *"Sri Krishna Tulabaram"* using innuendoes and insinuations, he played the role of Narada so well that the audience thought Kanta Rao lived in the character of Narada. Ghantasala sang *'padyams'* and famous song *"Bhale Manchi Chauka Beraamu"* with

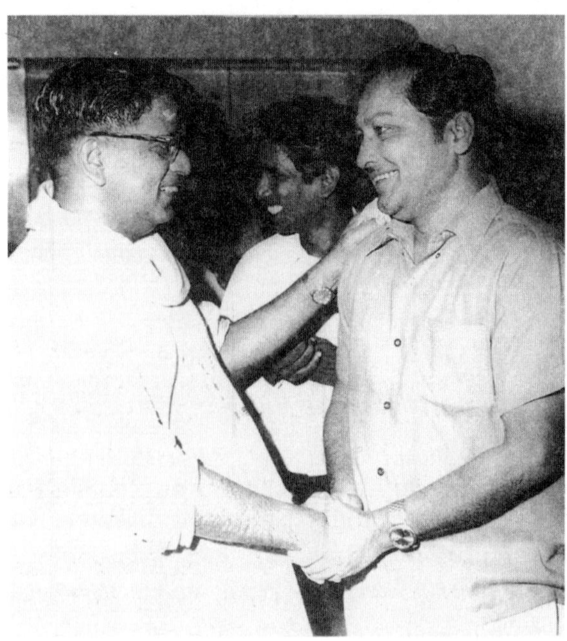

every nuance of emotion for Kanta Rao in the same movie. Though P. B. Srinivos sang a number of songs for Kanta Rao which suited him very well, Ghantasala also sang melodious songs for the veteran actor in a few historical periodic movies.

7. K. Jaggaiah

He was distinguished for his voice and dubbed for even renowned actor like Sivaji Ganeshan in about 100 movies. Though P. B. Srinivos was known as voice of Jaggaiah by singing memorable songs like *"Oho Gulabi Baala"*, Ghantasala too sang some melodious songs for Jaggaiah in movies like *"Padandi Munduku"* and *"Uyyala Jampala"*- notable among them is *"Kondagaali Tirigindi"*.

8. J. V. Ramanamurthy

He is an actor endowed with enviable theatrical talent. Whatever role was given to him- that of a hero, side hero or a character actor- he did justice to it. Ghantasala sang melodious songs for him like *"Payanniche Mana Valapula"*, *"Neeli Meghaalalo Gali Keratalalo"*, and *"Raave Naa Cheliya"*.

9. Haranath

He was a handsome actor who played the roles of mythological heroes like Sri Rama and Sri Krishna; his performances were next only to those of N. T. Rama Rao. Though P. B. Srinivos was the voice of Haranath by singing songs like *"Andala O Chiluka, Anduko Naa Lekha"* from "Letha Manasulu" and in rendering remarkable *'padyams'* like *"Chesina Karmaye Jeeviki Chukkani"*. Ghantasala too sang sonorous songs like *"Naa Chandamaama, Neeve Bhaama"*, which were pictured on Haranath.

10. Sobhan Babu

Though he started his career by playing small roles, Sobhan Babu rose to be a reckonable hero and played larger than life roles like that of *"Veerabhimanyu"*. Ghantasala's unbeatable melodies like *"Adigo Navalokam"*, *"Rambha Urvasi Thala Danne"*, *"Chuchi Valachi Chentaku Pilachi"* were pictured on Sobhan Babu. After Ghantasala's demise, S. P. Balu took over.

Ghantasala sang a few songs for younger actors like Krishna and Rammohan of which the prominent ones are *"Telugu Veera Levara"* and *"Divinunchi Bhuviki Digi Vachche digivachche"*.

NON TELUGU ACTORS

11. Shivaji Ganesan

He was one of the most popular actors in Southern India. Being a great fan of Ghantasala, Shivaji, in the initial stage, wanted Ghantasala to sing all the songs for him. He exceedingly liked the Telugu movie *"Chiranjeevulu"* and the music composed by Ghantasala for the movie. After the untimely demise of Ghantasala, Shivaji, consoling Savitramma, sat beside her for a day. He stood for old world values.

12. M. G. Ramachandran

He was also one of the most popular actors in Tamil film field. He founded AIADMK party, became powerful in Indian politics and was the Chief Minister of Tamil Nadu for 10 years (1977-87). He was also a great fan of Ghantasala and helped the credulous singer in Income tax matters.

DIRECTORS AND PRODUCERS

A number of directors and producers had a lot of respect for Ghantasala, encouraged him from the beginning of his career and extracted amazing work from him.

1. C. Krishnaveni

She was an actor, singer and producer rolled into one. When Ghantasala was a budding singer cum music director, Krishnaveni asked him to do the music composing for three of her movies *"Lakshmamma"*, *"Mana Desam"* and "Keelugurram". When some reporters and well wishers asked her why she took such a risk; she proclaimed: *"To me Ghantasala appeared to be a good, humble and polite person. I noticed divine qualities in him. It struck me that he would one day grow to be a genius in music"*.[5]

2. B. N. Reddy

He was a Dadashaheb Phalke award winner. He directed and produced movies like "Malleswari", *"Bangaru Papa"*, *"Rajamakutam"*, *"Rangula Raatnam"* and *"Bangaru Panjaram"*. He had a lot of affection and respect for Ghantasala and made him sing in all the movies produced by him. *"The Almighty has given a "Gandharva" as a gift to Telugu film field, that is Ghantasala,"* declared our Dadashaheb Phalke award winner.[6]

3. Chitoor V Nagaiah

He was known for his versatility: an actor, a singer, a music composer, a director and a producer rolled into one. He made Ghantasala sing his first film song in the movie *"Swargaseema"* for which he was the music composer. In a write up entitled *"Gandharvamsa Sambhutudu"*, Nagaiah stated emphatically: *"Some singers tune their voice to 'Shruti', whereas 'Shruti' itself is embedded in Ghantasala's voice. This is an amazing creative process, whenever Ghantasala sang a poem, sang a song, or sang a classical 'raaga', it will have 'bhaava' and 'laya' and it being pleasing, would enthrall the listeners. Another striking quality in Ghantasala is his humble and polite behavior"*. Nagaiah and Ghantasala sang together sonorously in movies like *"Tenali Ramakrishna"* and *"Poolarangadu"*. When Ghantasala was hesitating to lend his voice to a *'vidwan'* like Nagaiah for the movie *"Lava Kusa"*; Nagaiah told him *"You are also a vidwan. Don't hesitate. Sing for me"*.[7]

4. Balantrapu Rajanikantha Rao:

He was a multi talented person: he was a poet and playwright, singer and music composer rolled into one. As the Director of All India Radio, Rajani had the talent to identify talent: when Ghantasala was given only small roles in movies like 'Thyagayya', Rajani, having recognized the talent of the budding singer, made him sing in solos and groups, play roles in radio plays and compose music for poetic dramas.

5. Peketi Sivaram

'Vidwan eva vijanati vidwatjana parisramam/Nahi vandhya vijanati gurvi prasavavedana' (only a scholar can understand and appreciate another scholar's merit.) The same thing applies to every aspect of life. When an HMV officer rejected Ghantasala's voice being metallic, actor cum director Peketi Shivaram appreciated Ghantasala's singing abilities and got a mellifluous record produced on a padyam *"Nagumomu Naku Nishanadaa Bimbamu"* and a song *"Gaalilo Naa Bratuku Telipoyina Doyi"*. For the movies directed by Peketi later viz, *"Chuttarikalu"* and *"Bhale Abbayilu"*, Ghantasala

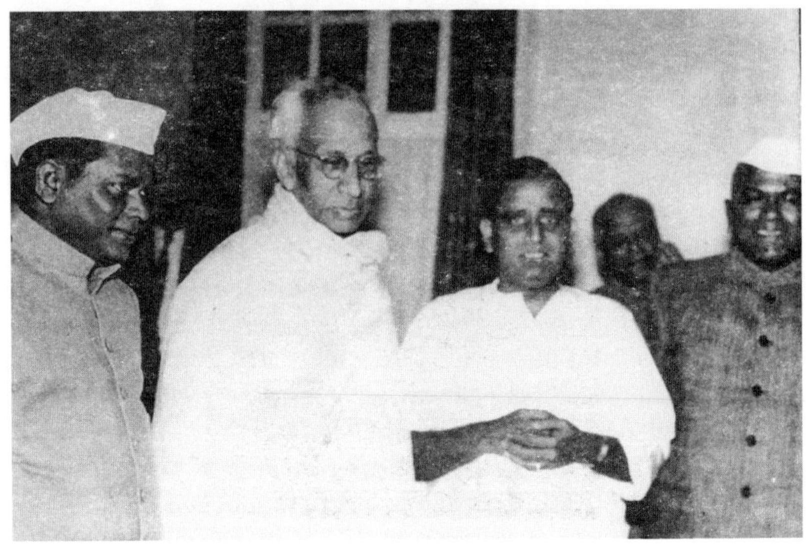

composed music. In the movie "Bhakta Raghunath" produced by Ghantasala, Peketi played a role.[8]

6. P. S. Ramakrishna

Along with his actor-wife P. Bhanumati, he founded the famous 'Bharani studios' and 'Bharani Pictures 'and produced a number of memorable movies: some of them are: *"Laila Majnu"*, *"Ratna-maala"*, *"Prema"*, *"Chandirani"*, *"Chakrapani"*, *"Vipranarayana"*, *"Chintamani"* and *"Batasari"*. Savitri Ghantasala in her book entitled Ghantasala Jnapakalu tells that P. Ramakrishna was fond of Ghantasala's voice and made him sing memorable songs in his movies. Even though P. Bhanumati used to put on airs, Ghantasala's and P. S. Ramakrishna's families were close to each other.[9]

7. Nagi Reddy and Chakrapani

Both of them were the key figures in the established of Vijaya productions and they produced movies like *"Chandraharam"*, *"Patala Bhairavi"*, *"Pellichesichudu"*, *"Mayabazar"*, *"Jagadeka Veeruni Katha"*, *"Gundamma Katha"*, and *"Appu Chesi Pappu Kudu"*. They were fond of Ghantasala and made him compose music for movies like *"Patala Bhairavi"*, *"Pellichesichudu"*, *"Mayabazar"*, and *"Gundamma Katha"*. They started a children's magazine called 'Chandamama' which was published in more than 10 languages. Chakrapani was a writer too.

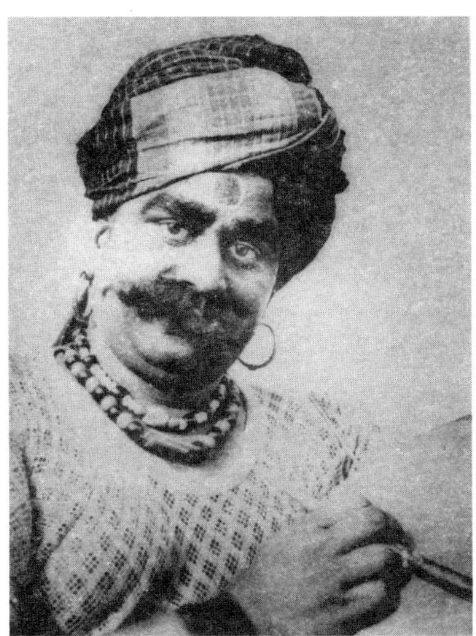

8. K. V. Reddy

Director cum producer K. V. Reddy was associated from the beginning i.e. since 1945 with classics like *"Swargaseema"*, *"Bhakta Potana"*, *"Yogi Vemana"*. His film *"Donga Ramudu"* was on the curriculum of Film and Television Institute of India (FTII) and his *"Patala Bhairavi"* got critical acclaim at India International Film Festival in 1952. The movie *"Mayabazaar"* was his magnum opus. He directed or produced films in which Ghantasala sang several sonorous songs.

9. L. V. Prasad

He was the founder of Prasad Art Productions and had played an important role in Telugu, Tamil and Hindi film industries. He was given the Dadasaheb Phalke award in 1982. Ghantasala was the music composer for some of the movies directed by Prasad, namely *"Manadesham"*, *"Shavukaru"* and *"Pellichesichudu"*. In some other movies directed by L. V. Prasad –namely, *"Samsaram"* and *"Appuchesipapaukudu"*, Ghantasala sang memorable songs.

10. Kamalakara Kameswara Rao

He directed more than 50 films in Telugu, Tamil and Hindi. He was called *'Pauranika Chitra Brahma'*. His movies *"Mahakavi Kalidas"*, *"Mahamantri Timmarusu"*, *"Nartanasala"*, *"Pandavavanavasam"*, and *"Gundamma Katha"* achieved critical

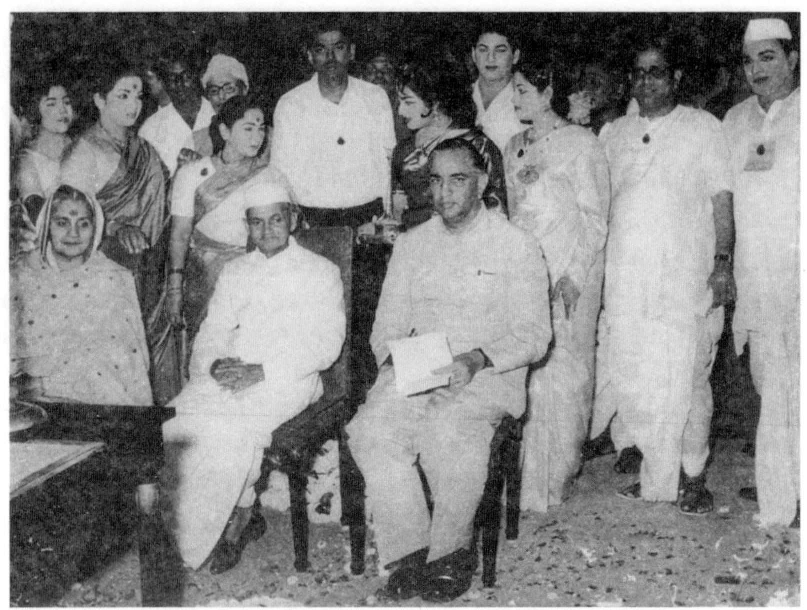

acclaim as well as commercial success. In most of the movies directed by K. Kameeswara Rao, Ghantasala sang excellent songs and *'padyams'*.

11. D. Madhusudana Rao

He was a producer and screen play writer endowed with an in- depth knowledge of music. Along with Akkineni Nageswara Rao, he founded 'Annapurna Pictures' and produced movies like *"Donga Ramudu"*, *"Velugu Needalu"*, *"Maangalyabalam"*, *"Dr. Chakravarthy"* and *"Chaduvukunna Ammayilu"*. He had a lot of affection and respect for Ghantasala as he was aware that due to the impressive songs sung by the great singer, his movies got more and more profits.[10]

12. V. B. Rajendra Prasad

He produced a number of movies in Telugu, Tamil and Hindi. Some of the prominent ones are: *"Aaraadhana"*, *"Anthasthulu"*, *"Aatmabalam"*, *"Aastiparulu"*, and *"Dasarabullodu"*. Ghantasala sang a number of melodious songs in those movies. Like D. Madhusudana Rao, Rajendra Prasad too knew the value of Ghantasala and gave him substantial remuneration.[11]

13. D. V. S. Raju

He was a share holder in N. T. Rama Rao's National Art Theatres. Raju had a lot of affection and respect for Ghantasala. In the movies produced by Raju, Ghantasala sang mellifluous songs. Those are: *"Mangamma Shapatham", "Gandikota Rahasyam"* etc.

14. Sundarlal Nahata

He played a key role in Chamriya Talkie Distributors and Rajasri Distributors. For all the 10 movies produced by Nahata, Ghantasala composed music. Those are *"Jayam Manade", "Manchi Manasuku Manchi Rojulu", "Sati Anasuya", "Shanti Nivasam", "Shabhash Ramudu", "Abhimanam", "Shabhash Raja", "Rakta Sambandham", "Bandipotu" and "Gudigantalu"*. Nahata, obviously, had a lot of affection and respect for Ghantasala. But, whenever Nahata wanted the reputed composer to adapt the tunes of some popular Hindi songs - like in *"Shanti Nivasam"*, Ghantasala – being reluctant to copy the tunes composed by other composers – would ask his assistant J. V. Raghavulu to compose music for those songs. Notable among them is *"Come Come Come Kangaroo Neekelane"*.[12]

15. Kovelamudi Bhaskar Rao

He was the proprietor of Bhaskar productions. Out of respect for Ghantasala he made the reputed composer to compose music for all his movies. Those are *"Bratuku Teruvu", "Cherapakura Chedevu", "Repu Needi", "Parvati Kalyanam"* and *"Mohini Rukmangada"*.

16. K. Gopal Rao

He was the proprietor of Ashwaraj Pictures. He produced two mythological movies, *"Vinayaka Chavithi"* and *"Deepavali"*, for which Ghantasala composed music. One of the most memorable devotional song of Ghantasala period was *"Dinakara Shubhakara Deva"* in *"Deepavali"*, Madhavapeddi and A. P. Komala meticulously sang *"Sarasajakshi Yakshaganam"* under the able guidance of Ghantasala. A. P. Komala's *"Sariya Naato"* sang pictured on Mahanati Savitri emits the nuances of Satyabhama's confidence and ego.

17. Tota Subba Rao

He was the proprietor of Sridevi Productions. He produced movies like *"Paramanandayya Sishyula Katha", "Bhuvana Sundari Katha", "Peddakkayya", "Chuttarikalu"*, and *"Pattindalla*

Bangaram". Ghantasala composed music for all these movies and some of them became commercial as well as musical hits.

18. K. Vishwanath:

He is one of the well known film directors in Southern Indian Film Field. He directed/produced a number of movies dealing with human and social issues. Some of his well known movies are *"Shankarabharanam"*, *"Sagarasangamam"*, *"Swarna Kamalam"*, *"Swati Mutyam"*, and *"Swati Kiranam"*. He has high regard and admiration for Ghantasala. In the book 'Mee Ghantasala', he says that as a recordist, he was fortunate enough to arrange the mike a number of times before Ghantasala. [13]

Notes

1. Mee Ghantasala, *p*. 39
2. Ibid, *p*. 42
3. 'Parakaya *p*ravesham' is the act of a sadhak's prana or consciousness leaving his body and entering a dead man's or animal body. The sadhak's consciousness can get back to his original body if it is kept safe.
4. Ghantasala Jnapakalu, *p*. 82
5. Ibid, *p*. 197
6. Mee Ghantasala, *p*. 99
7. Ibid, *p*. 100
8. Ibid, *p*. 35
9. Ghantasala Jnapakalu, *p*. 44
10. Ibid, *p*. 136
11. Ibid, *p*. 137
12. Ibid, *p*. 143
13. Mee Ghantasala, *p*. 48

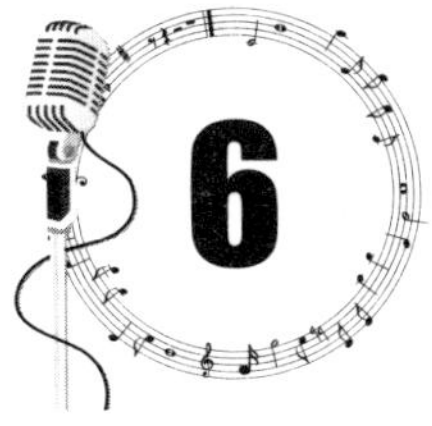

The Indelible Impact of an Immortal singer

I Ghantasala's Human and Humane qualities:

"How deeply you touch another life is how rich your life is"

– Sadguru Vasudev of Isha Foundation

"To be meek, patient, tactful, modest, honorable, and brave is not to be either manly or womanly; it is to be humane"

– Jane Harrison, British Writer

"Ghantasala's genius as a music composer lies in the fact that he composed music keeping in mind the common man. As a singer he made modifications to the pronunciation, which made the song more acceptable to the audiences. That should sound sweet was his aim. His simplicity endeared him to everybody"

– VAK Rangarao,
Art critic and Music Historian

The extremely valuable tribute is that which is paid by one's collegues and competitors. Stalwarts like R. Balasaraswati Devi, P. Leela, P. Susheela, Jikki, S. Janaki, P. B. Srinivos and Patrayani Sangeeta Rao were all praise for Ghantasala's magnanimity and munificence. On the contrary to the pusillaminity and pettiness generally prevalent in Indian film field, Ghantasala was magnanimous towards his collegues as well as juniors. To vouch for this, the following facts will be referred to as evidence (In some cases the affection and regard were mutual)

i. When the rehersals of the songs for 'Malleswari 'were taking place, Ghantasala went into raptures observing the marvelous singing skills of the composer S. Rajeswara Rao. Reciprocating this magnamous jesture, it seems S. Rajeswara Rao said "What ever comes from Ghantasala's voice is golden; people crave for it".[1]

ii. For the movie 'Vayyaribhama', S. Rajeswara Rao was the music composer; as he was ill, he could not make the tunes for some songs. As the release of the movie was getting delayed, Ghantasala prepared the tunes for four songs and got them recorded in 1953. In the titles, only S. Rajeswara Rao's name appeared.[2]

iii. For the movie 'Mayabazar' S. Rajeswara Rao was initially the music composer; he prepared only tunes but not music for 4 songs; he abandoned the work being at loggerheads with Nagireddy and Chakrapani; later, having been requested by Chakrapani, Ghantasala became the music composer for 'Mayabazar'; After retaining the tunes made by S. Rajeswara Rao for the four songs, the singer-composer composed mesmerizing tunes and music not only for songs but also for 'padyams' and also background music; when he wanted S. Rajeswara Rao's name to be included in the titles, Chakrapani did not agree to his proposal.[3]

iv. Ghantasala recommended freshers like S. P. Balasubramanium and V. Ramakrishna to his fellow music composers. He made S. P. Balu sing in the movie 'Tulasi' for which he composed music.[4]

v. As M. S. Ramarao at one point of time was facing financial problems, the singer composer made him sing the songs which he was assigned to sing.[5]

vi. As music composer Ashwatthama was facing financial problems, Ghantasala gave up the music composing of the movie 'Mayani – Mamata' in favour of his friend.[6]

vii. For financially helping the orchestra troupe he did many 'kacheries' – sometimes without payment for himself.

viii. He started Musicians' Association and was responsible for getting a musician's building contructed on Arcot road, Madras.[7]

For the aforementioned reasons, the versatile actor Gummadi said; "I have high regard for two persons in the film field – One is Nagaiah and another Ghantasala."[8]

"Janmana Jayate Shudrah I
Karmana Jayate Brahmanah II"

– A Vedic aphorism

Even though Ghantasala belonged to a traditional Hindu/ Brahmin family, he did not follow the conventions of a typical Brahmin family. He did not keep the Harijans or Christians or Muslims away from him. Being a follower of Mahatma Gandhi and real Vedic Dharma, he treated all human beings as equal and never discriminated them on the basis of caste or creed. Around 1948 his accountant was a harijan boy; the singer – composer had lunches/ dinners sitting beside him. The famous poet Jashua was a Christian; when he hesitated to sit beside the pious Brahmin, the latter made

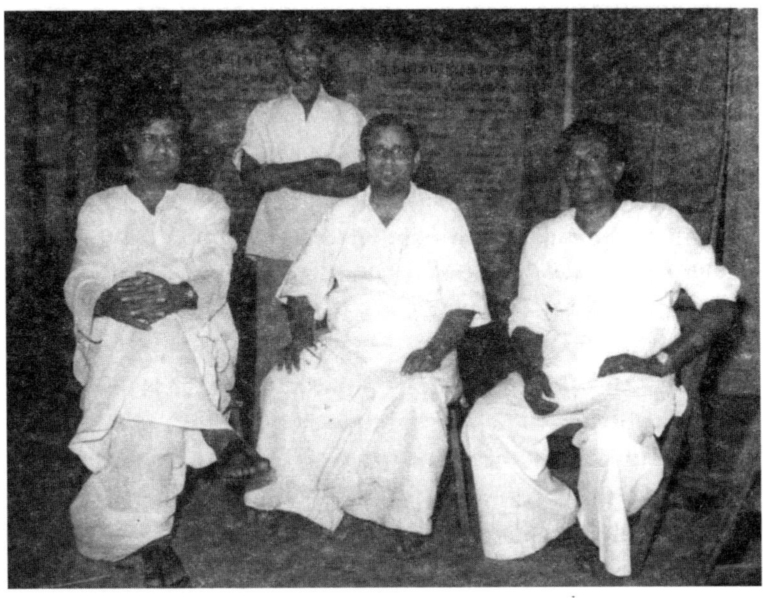

him sit beside him. The famous Hindustani musician Bade Gulam Ali Khan stayed in the upper floor of Ghantasala's house for months together during his trips to Madras. Ghantasala never objected to the Hindustani singer eating non vegetarian food in his house. [9]

All his colleagues without exception vouch for the fact that Ghantasala was an embodiment of humility, politeness and simplicity. He never told anybody – including his wife Savitramma- that he was a great singer. He listened to the guidelines given by every music composer – including his juniors like Pamarthi, Raghavulu and Pandit Janardan. The sitar maestro has told me that while he was composing music for the songs to be sung by Ghantasala, the great singer politely listened to him and followed the guidelines given by him.[10]

II Ghantasala's triumphant sojourn abroad:

Sir Sarvepalli Radhakrishnan, the President of India (1962-1967) was fond of Ghantasala's songs and his singing skills. He wanted Ghantasala to get International recognition. The Philosopher-President's words made a profound impact on Ghantasala's mind; as a result the singer-composer was determined to go abroad and spread Telugu songs and Southern Indian classical tunes in foreign lands for the benefit of foreigners as well as Indians living abroad.[11]

After collecting funds from different sources Ghantasala and his 10- member team left Meenambakam airport, Madras on 7 October 1971. Cutting across the linguistic barriers, the entire film field of Madras actors, singers, music-composers, lyricists, directors, producers and scores of technicians and admirers went to the airport to see off the famous singer-composer. When the flight reached Bangalore, the Kannada film industry and admirers saw him off at Jalahalli airport. The Andhra association of Bombay organized a big function in honour of Ghantasala and saw him and his team off at Santacruz airport. Their flight left for West Germany.[12]

West Germany trip: The immortal singer's first concert abroad took place in Gottengen city's Institute of Pedagogia. Of the 1000 people who attended the concert, 90% were Germans and the rest were Asians. They liked our music in general. At the end of the concert, Ghantasala's rendition of 'Raghupati Raghava Rajaram' and 'Hare Rama Hare Krishna'mesmerized the Germans. The program, which was planned for 2 hours and a half, had to be extended to 4 hours. Many German students went to the railway station to see Ghantasala off; Some Indian admirers went to Frankfurt airport also. Among the Germans, Kurt Weber became an ardent admirer of Ghantasala, carried his baggage in Gottengen and he came to India too.[13]

A German musician wrote the following in a newspaper published in Germany. This is the English translation of what Mr. Reinhard Kunz said:

"Amnesty International could hardly have (arranged) offered a better programme of entertainment to the music lovers of Gottengen than to invite Ghantasala, the king of songs, from South India, to give a concert in the assembly hall of the Institute of pedagogies Gottingen. The good cause in question was the aid to the refuges from Pakistan. The proceeds of the evening go to them and the amount must have been high considering (the fact) that Ghantasala sang without any remuneration and the hall was almost filled to capacity.

The programme included selections ranging from the classical period of Indian Philosophy upto contemporary film music. All those who attended the concert which went on till close on midnight would agree that the concert held the audience spell bound right through. This was not only due to the fascinating virtuosity with

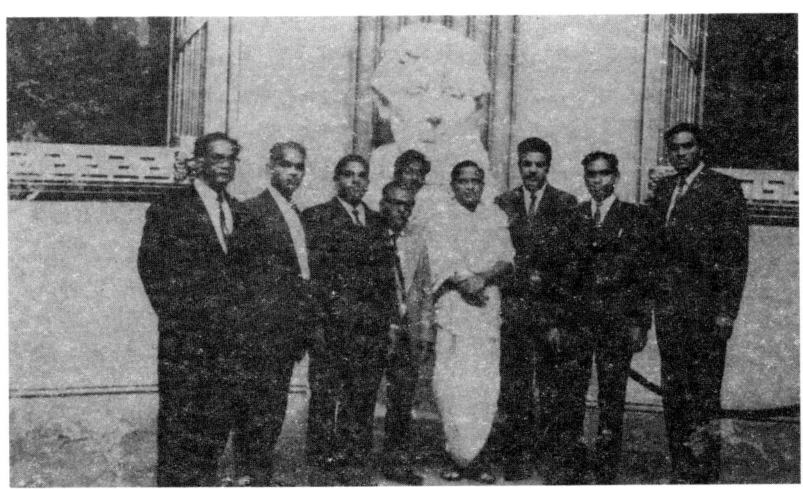

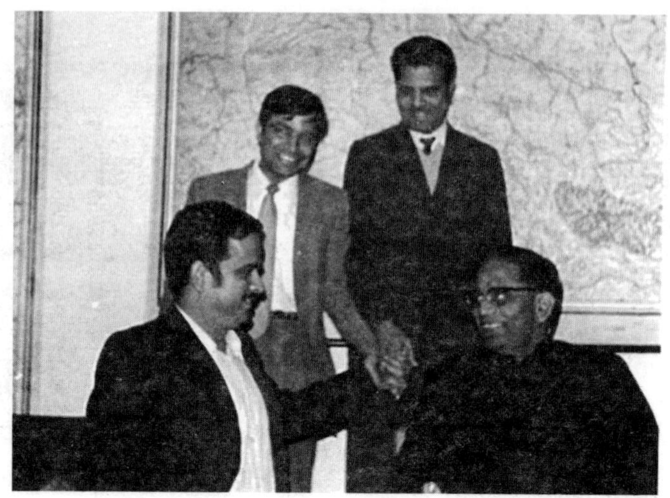

which Ghantasala negotiated the requiems of $^{1}/_{4}{}^{th}$ and $^{1}/_{8}{}^{th}$ tones of the n harmonic range of notes, but also due to the instrumentalists among the ensemble who were completely on par with the signer through their perfect mastery over their instruments. The Sitar and flute (solos) as well as the concerned effort of all the percussion instruments of the ensemble belonged to the highlights of the concert and brought great ovation from the audience".[14]

London Trip: Tanguturi Surya Kumari, a niece of Tanguturi Prakasam Panthulu, was the hostess in London. She organized a concert of Ghantasala in her School of Dance. About 200 attended the concert. The audience wanted to come to London again and again for performing concerts.[15]

USA and Canada trip: The concerts of Ghantasala and his team were held in NewYork, Wasington DC, Los Angeles, SanFrancisco, Chicago, Detroit, Boston, Syracuse and Toranto. At every place the program was as follows: Ghantasala started the concert with devotional and classical songs; it was followed by Pandit Janardan's sitar performance; then Ghantasala sang popular songs in Telugu, Tamil, Kannada, Malayalam and Hindi; after the break, Nerella Venu Madhav did mimicry; it was followed by Nanjundiah's flute performance; at the end Ghantasala sang folk songs, 'Raghupati Raghava Rajaram' and 'Hare Rama Hare Krishna'. On 28 October 1971, Ghantasala's concert was held in Dag Hamarskjold Hall of the

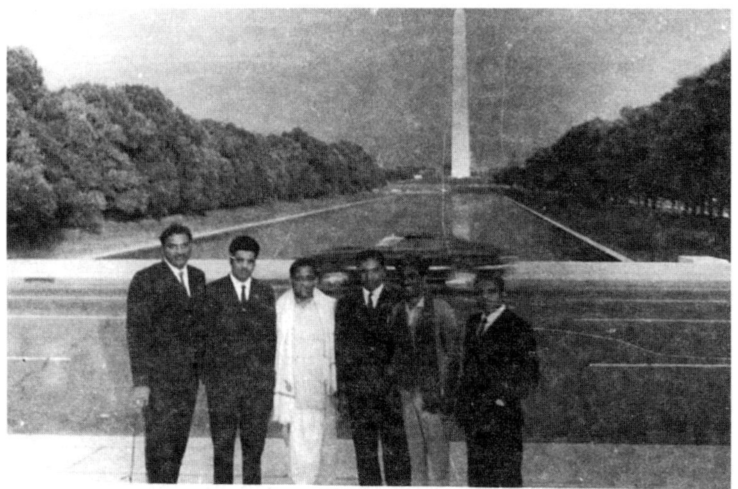

United Nations Organization. The diplomats of various countries attended the concert. As a mark of their appreciation, they presented him with a"Peace Medal.' That was one of the biggest honors received by the singer-composer in his life. The program, at every place, had to be extended from 3 to 4 hours. Every where paens of praise were conferred on Ghantasala and his team. The singer composer was invariably asked to perform again and again at different places. It was indeed a triumphant sojourn.[16] He had a stop over in Paris and Kuwait, but he did not perform concerts in those two places.

III Perpetuation of Ghantasala's memory:

"Ghantasala was a multi faceted talent and he will always be remembered for his unparrelled contribution to music"

– Bharat Ratna Lata Mangeshkar

"Ghantasala is alive. He is alive in the hearts of music lovers. As long as Telugu culture is alive, Telugu music is alive, he will be alive."

– A. Nageshwara Rao

"Volumes can be written on Ghantasala. He is immortal- He is immortal- He is immortal."

– S. Janaki

At least four generations have been enjoying Ghantasala's songs. He has made millions and millions of people enjoy the nectar of his music. Even 40years after his demise, on Tirumala Hill, in railway junctions, in tea/coffee shops and on trains, one will find devotees, labourers and even beggars singing his songs for getting some solace. His ardent admirers started fan clubs in every district of Telugu states – even in Tamilnadu, Karnataka and Odisha. They have been celebrating Ghantasala's birth and death anniversaries by singing his songs for days together. Vamsi Rama Raju started Ghantasala International Foundation Trust (GIFT) and conducted 'Ghantasala Aradhanotsvas' for 51 days which got into Limca Book of Records. Vamsi Rama Raju through GIFT organizes every year in the USA the 'Aradhanotsvas' of Ghantasala. On Ghantasala's name websites have appeared in the internet for discussing the songs and music of Ghantasala; among them www.ghantasala.info is popular.[17]

Ghantasala's fans were creative and innovative. Dr. Syed Rahamtullah was born and brought up in Odisha. His fondness for Telugu language and admiration for Ghantasala are enviable. He created a new genre called 'Sangeetavadhanam'. In this genre, they can be 20 people (pruchchakas) who put questions related to Ghantasala i.e. his life, his producers and directors, the release dates of the movies for which he composed music, the ragas on which his songs were based, the beginning of a particular song or its middle, his private songs et cetera. Dr. Rahamtulla meticulously gives appropriate answers within the given time limit.

Another innovative approach is that of Lalitha Sindoori. She is basically a Kuchipudi dancer. Besides performing the traditional Kuchipudi dance items, she took up the onerous task of making choreography and dancing for Ghantasala's private folk songs and classical songs like'Ashtapadis.'She received the acclaim of the chief minister of Andhra Pradesh abd the Kuchipudi maestro Sobha Naidu.[18]

There are 32 statues of Ghantasala in different parts of India. Those are: Parlakhemdi, Orissa, Vijayanagaram, Saluru, Visakhapatnam, Parawada, Ananthapalli, Thadepalligudem, Bheemavaram, Kakinada, Rajahmundry, Vijayawada (2) Guntur, Gudiwada, Chowtapally, Machilipatnam, Srikakulam, Cuddapah, Nellore, Ongole,

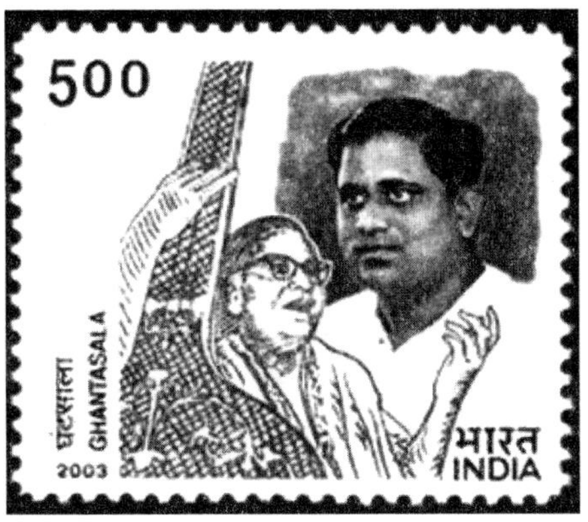

Chittor, Markapuram Tirupati (2), Tekupalli, Tenali, Palakollu, Hyderabad (2) Ghantasala, Kurnool, Venkatagiri, Aakiveedu (under installation)

It appears that no other artist in the world received such an honour. The initiative for installing the first statue of Ghantasala in Hyderabad was taken by the popular singer S. P. Bala Subramaniam. On 14 Febraury 1993 Bharat Ratna Lata Mangeshkar inaugurated it.[19]

IV The significance of being Ghantasala:

In a meeting held in Madras in 1964, Ghantasala reiterated his views on how the *'Kritis'* of Carnatic music should be rendered: It is wrong to condemn the attitude of the people if the attendance at the *'Kacheries'* of cinema songs is more than the attendance at classical music concerts. Musicians have to ruminate over the circumstances and the situations in which *'Nadabrahma Tyagaraja'* wrote and sang those *'Kritis'*; how the *'Vaggeyakara'* expressed the anguish of his heart and how profoundly it reflected in his *'Kritis'*, instead of displaying their expertise in the mechanics of musicology."[20] Ghantasala practiced whatever he stated in the meeting; he never neglected *'Sahitya'* at the expense of *'Sangeet'* Stalwarts like Pendyala, P. Susheela and Sangeeta Rao in one voice proclaimed that Ghantasala was the only singer at the national level who could sing melodiously at all the three *'Sthayees'* - i.e. 'Mandra, Madhyama and Tara 'sthayees'. In the preceding chapters we have seen how Ghantasala sang mellifluously the songs and rendered the 'Padyams' based on classical ragas. We have also seen how the 'Nav rasaas' and the tenth rasa 'Bhakti' reflected in his songs as well as 'Padyams'. A stalwart in Carnatic Music, Nedunuri Krishnamu murthy declared'---Ghantasala can easily perform a three-hour concert in carnatic music; it is the fortune of film field that he entered it and shone like the Sun. In the pauranic movies like 'Lavakusa' and 'Rahasyam' the songs based on classical ragas are "praise worthy."[21] Some other stalwarts in Carnatic Music also like Chittoor Subramanya Pillai, Tyagaraja Bhagavatar and Nukala Chinna Satyanarayana discussed Ghantasala's expertise in and contribution to classical music. A musician of the stature of T.M.Krishna declared that Ghantasala was a "Classically trained singer who got into playback singing."[22] Nukala Chinna Satyanarayana and Sangeeta Rao proclaimed that Ghantasala's songs could be used for teaching classical ragas.[23]

His admirers commemorated Ghantasala by naming the Music College in Vijayawada as Ghantasala Venkateswara Rao Government Music College.

The analysis *ut infra* by a non-Telugu speaking musician reemphasizes the above discussion.

Mr. Khan from Madhya Pradesh – who had an experience of about 35 years in the field of Classical music, wrote the following in his email dated 31 May 2010.[24]

Khan said:

"There are ragas which require display of soft, sweet, velvet voice and ragas which require display of hard and rough voice, ragas which require majestic and resonating voice display, Ragas which require majestic and resonating voice display, dynamism etc... and depending upon the various ragas the voice culture has to undergo a change along with the expressions. Even Mohammad Rafi Sahab's voice is mostly uniform and of same type in all his songs. Even the ragas which require rough voice and hard voice to be used, Rafi Sahab displays his soft voice only because his voice belonged to that type. That is why many music directors, depending upon compositions and various ragas, prefer various singers depending upon their voice culture. This is the main reason for preferring various types of singers by various music directors for various types of songs and ragas. This is where I find the difference between Ghantasala Sahab and other singers.

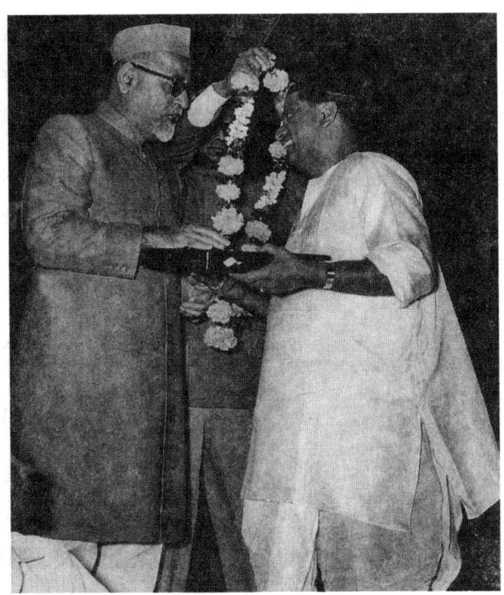

This is what is called as perfect technical ability. He sounds sweet wherever it is required and only to the extent it is required, nothing more, nothing less (his rendition of the Bhoop and Kalyan ragas is indeed exactly sweet and the rendition in Bhimpalas and Sohani ragas is indeed dynamic and majestic – a perfection par excellence). That is INDEED a god gifted voice. Similar things apply to other things i.e. expression and change in voice culture (and this is one of the main areas where Rafi Sahab falls back behind Ghantasala Sahab). That is the highest quality as per pure music rule. A perfect musician, will thus, obviously prefer Ghantasala Sahab over Rafi Sahab and other playback singers."

I have seen many people who say that they like only sweet voices which sound melodious in general; in my view, it is clear that such people really do not have the proper taste of music, as it is known that sweet voice has to be used only for certain sweet ragas like bloop, bhilawal thaat, kalyan etc."

Nava Rasas [25]

1. Sringaara
    a. *"Himagiri Sogasulu"*... Paandava Vanavasam
    b. *"Muripinche Andaale"*... Bobbili Yuddham

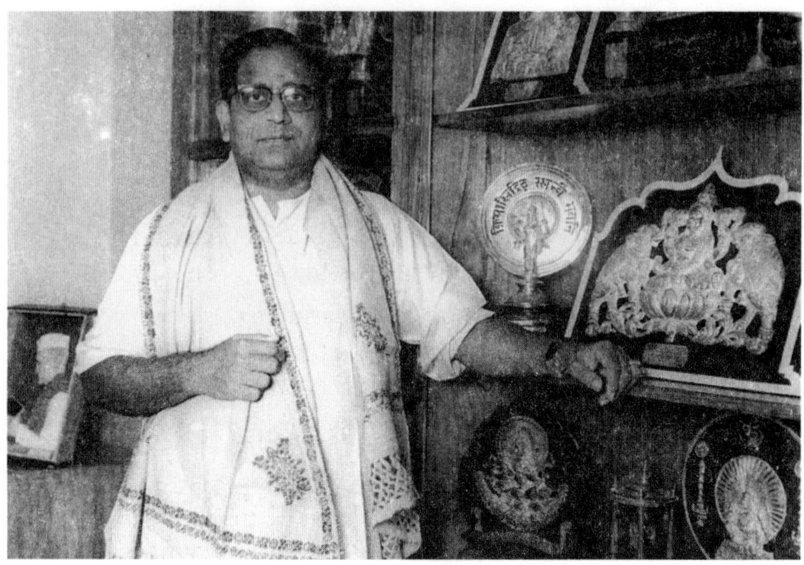

   c. *"Enta Ghatu Premayo"*... Patala Bhairavi
   d. *"Naa Chandamama Neeve Bhama"*... Paandava Vanavasam
2. Haasya
   a. *"Yelli Naato Sarasa"*... Bhuvanasundari Kadha
   b. *"Sundari Neevanti"*... Maya Bazaar
   c. *"Premo Premo Prema"*... Cherapakuraa Chedevu
   d. *"Kasi Ki Poyanu Ramahari"*... Appuchesi Pappu Kodu
3. Karuna
   a. *"Bangaru Bomma"*... Chadarangam
   b. *"Yenta Manchidaanavamma"*... Kannatalli
   c. *"Pushpavilapam"*... Private Song
   "Kuntikumari"... Private Song
4. Roudra
   a. *"Dhaaruni Raajya Sampada"* (Padyam)... Pandava Vanavasam
   b. *"Dharani Garbhamu"* (Padyam)... Sri Krishnaarjuna Yudham
   c. *"Jayatvadadabhra Vibhrama Bhrama"*... Sitarama Kalyanam
5. Veera
   a. *"Telugu Veera"* Alluri Seeta Ramaraju

   b. *"Le Lendoi Le Lendoi"*... Private song
   c. *"Jayam Manade Jayam Manade"*... Private Song
6. Bhayaanaka Bheebhatsa
   a. *"Adigo Alladigo"*... Sri Krishnavataram
7. Adbhuta
   a. *"Oho Divya Ramanulaara"*... Jagadeka Veeruni Kadha
   b. *"Shilala Pai"*... Manchi Manasulu
   c. *"Yevarivo Nee Yevarivo"*... Punarjanma
   d. *"Manikya Veenam"*... Mahakavi Kalidas
8. Shanta
   a. *"Sandeehinchaku Mamma"*... Lavakusa
   b. *"Idi Mana Aashramambu"*... Lavakusa
9. Shoka
   a. *"Amma Ani Arachina"*... Panduranga Mahatmyam
   b. *"Raanika Neekosam"*... Maayani Mamatha
   c. *"Bommanu Chesi"*... Devata
   d. *"Jagame Maya Bratuke Maya"... Devadas*
10. Bhakti
   a. *"Sesha Sailaavasa"*... Venkateshwara Mahatmyam
   b. *"Mahesha Paapa Vinaasaa"*... Kaala Hasthi Mahatmyam
   c. *"Kaanarara Kailasa Nivasa"*... Sitarama Kalyanam
   d. *"Edukondala Sami"*... Private Song

Besides the aforementioned scholarly statements, we can clearly see that Ghantasala could sing songs or Padyams in all the Nav Rasas and the tenth rasa Bhakti whereas an admirable playback singer like Mohammad Rafi-who is comparable to Ghantasala in terms of quality of voice and range of singing-did not sing in rasas like 'Bhayanak, Bhibhatsa and Roudra' as those rasas were conspicuously absent in Hindi film music. Stalwarts-with enviable expertise in classical as well as light music-like Pendyala, P. Susheela and Sangeeta Rao have proclaimed in one voice that Ghantasala sang melodiously in all the three Sthayees-Mandra, Madhyama and Tara sthayees. He sang more than 10,000 songs, padyams and stotras inTelugu, Tamil, Kannada, Malayalam, Hindi, Sinhalese and Sanskrit. Even music composers, singers and directors of astounding expertise in Hindi film field like

Lata Mangeshkar, Mohammad Rafi, Naushad Ali and V. Shantaram have conferred encomiums on Ghantasala.[26] It all proves that Ghantasala is the Epitome of Tradition and The Individual Talent.

Notes

1. Ghantasala Jnapakalu, *p*. 61
2. ibid, *p*. 62
3. Ibid, PP 64–65
4. Ibid, *p*. 167
5. Ibid, *p*. 164
6. Ibid, *p*. 64
7. Ibid, *pp*. 168–169
8. Ibid, *p*. 82
9. Ibid, *p*. 75
10. In a personal interview held in June 2016, Pandit Janardan told me this.
11. Ghantasala Jnapakalu, *p*. 145
12. Ibid, *p*. 151
13. Ibid, *p*. 151–152
14. Ibid, P.207
15. Ibid, *p*. 153
16. Mee Ghantasala, pp 135–136
17. Ghantasala Jnapakalu, *p*. 225.
18. Ibid, *p*. 224–225
19. Dr. K. V. Rao-Veera Veeraabhimani of Ghantasala-gave me this information
20. Ghantasala
21. Mee Ghantasala *p*. 117
22. A Southern Music. *p*. 259
23. Mee Ghantasala *p*. 89
24. Ghantasala Jnapakalu, P. 215–216
25. S. V. Ramana Murthy gave me this information.
26. Ghantasala Jnapakalu.

Annexure I: Tamil songs

S. No	Name of the Tamil song	Name of the movie
1	AadiPaadi	Engaveettu Mahalakshmi
2	Aadumayil	Kalaivaanan
3	AahaEnbani	Mayabazar
4	Aagaaya Veethiyil	Manjal Mahimai
5	Amaithiyillathen Maname	Pathaala Bhairavi
6	AmmaAmmaEnum	Manaalane Mangaiyin Bhagyam
7	AmmaNeekalangade	Kanavane Kan Kanda Deivam
8	AnandamYede	Chenchu Lakshmi
9	AnbeYenRaja	Chenchu Lakshmi
10	Andanal(Padyam)	Chenchu Lakshmi
11	Aswamedayagam	LavaKusa
12	BharatiDevi	Niraparathi
13	Brundavana	Vazhkai Oppantham
14	Chittitalam	Gundasundari Kathai
15	DumDumYenKalyanam	Mayabazar
16	Ellam Inbamayam	Ellam Inbamayam
17	EnimayaanaSamsaarame	Parobakaram
18	EnnaSiksha	Chandraharam
19	Ennathan	Pathaala Bhairavi
20	Gundupota revolver	Mamiyarum Oru Veettu Marumagal
21	Idavavil	Lyla Majnu
22	Idayavani	Vazhkai Oppantham

S. No	Name of the Tamil song	Name of the movie
23	IluvarNayagan	LavaKusa
24	InbaKaviya	Kaadhal
25	IndaVulaga	Gundasundari Kathai
26	JalJalJal	Swarna Manjari
27	JayaJayaSriRama	LavaKusa
28	Jeevitamellam	Kaadhal
29	Jodimaatta	Parobakaram
30	Kaadale	Pathaala Bhairavi
31	KadalNilave	Arasaala pirandhavan
32	Kalleyan	Karthavarayani kathai
33	Kalyanam Aagum Munne	Puthuyugam
34	KalyeSaradaDevi	Kalaivaanan
35	Kanavithuthan	Devadas
36	Kanintha	Anarkali
37	Kanivudan	Vazhkai Oppantham
38	KannudanKalandhidum	Mayabazar
39	KanPaarvai	Amara Deepam
40	KarileSavari	Engaveettu Mahalakshmi
41	Kavipadum	Bhagyadevathai
42	Kodaimaraindal	Manjal Mahimai
43	Krishnaa	Pennin Perumai
44	Maadapura	NattiyaThara
45	MaalaiNeratile	Kalaivaanan
46	Maanmadi	Lyla Majnu
47	MaaradhaSogamdhano	Manjal Mahimai

S. No	Name of the Tamil song	Name of the movie
48	Malarodum	Jayasimha
49	MalarumNeeye	Amara Deepam
50	Mangayindan	Jayasimha
51	Manivasitha	Chenchu Lakshmi
52	MannukeeduPonkeetal	Kalvanin Kathali
53	Marattil	Chenchu Lakshmi
54	Mevitamellam	Kadhal
55	Mudiyadu	Rajasevai
56	Mutthuku	Anbu Sahotharagal
57	NankondaKadal	Kadhal
58	NeedaneLogamu	Vazhkai Oppantham
59	NeedaneYannadye	Lyla Majnu
60	Needhaana	Mayabazar
61	NeeYeYanValvi	Kalaivaanan
62	OAnarkali	Anarkali
63	OhDevadas	Devadas
64	OhoBrahmadevane	Gundasundari Kathai
65	OhoVenilave	Prema Pasam
66	ParandhuSellum	Lyla Majnu
67	Poodusellayo	Rajasevai
68	Podakavayya	Mayabazar
69	Rajasekhara	Anarkali
70	SandehamuYenamma	LavaKusa
71	Santosham	Devadas
72	Seva	Navajeevanam

S. No	Name of the Tamil song	Name of the movie
73	SiripadiNilave	Amara Deepam
74	Soninatha	Devadas
75	SrihariDeva	Chenchu Lakshmi
76	Suyanalamperitha	Yaar paiyan
77	SwagatamSwagatam	Nirdoshi
78	Tannudan	Mayabazar
79	Thesulavude	Manalane Mangayin Baakiyam
80	ThulliThulli	NattiyaThara
81	Tuninta pan maname	Devadas
82	Ulagemayam	Devadas
83	UllasamSedum	Tenali Raman
84	UllasaUlagam	Alibabavum 40 Thirundnagalum
85	Uravam	Devadas
86	Uttaman	Sampoorna Ramayanam
87	UyirudanUnnaikaanbeno	Paadaala Bhairavi
88	Vaanmethiley	Chandi Rani
89	Vaarayadaye	Vazhkai Oppantham
90	Vaarayo	Lyla Majnu
91	VaazhvinJeevan	Andaman Kaithi
92	Varujyothidyvam	Chandraharam
93	Varungaala bharatha veera	Kalyanam Panni paar
94	VazhvileKanavupalikumo	Chandraharam
95	Vengale	Maataum Pitharuvum Munnari Daivam
96	VenniladJyothiyai	Manamagan Thevai

S. No	Name of the Tamil song	Name of the movie
97	Veyiluketra Nizhalundu_ Duet	Kalvanin Kaadhali
98	Veyiluketra Nizhalundu_ Solo	Kalvanin Kaadhali
99	Vinainaale Vantha	Aasai Magan
100	Vinaiya vithiya	Kathal
101	Vulakkagha	Mayabazar
102	Vurudan	Pathaala Bhairavi
103	VuyarTarunaMurty	Chenchu Lakshmi
104	YekaanthaNelayaale	Jayasimha
105	YenadhaaruyirVanithamani	Chandraharam
106	Yengethan	Amara Deepam
107	Yengumeanandam	Bhale Raman
108	Yevanandalu	Kalyanam Panni paar
109	Nenzame	Parobakaram

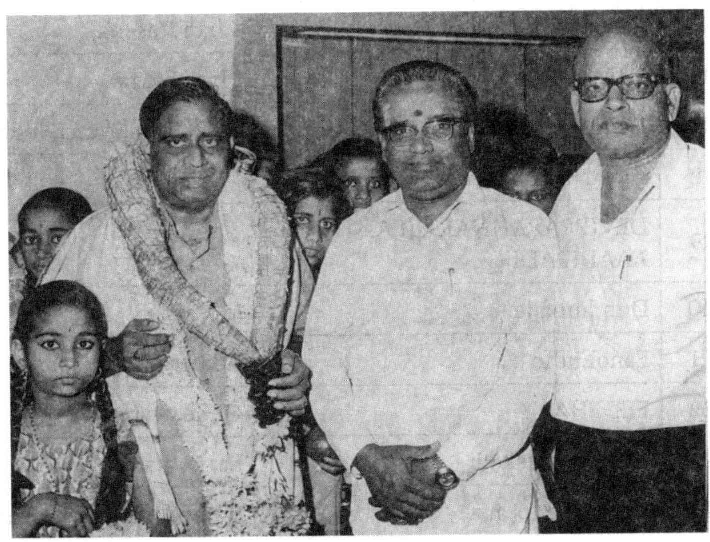

Annexure II
Kannada songs

S. No	Name of the Kannada song	Name of the movie
1	AadiPaadi	Sathi Shakti
2	Aadipujaye	
3	AasaYekasa	Jagadekaveerana Kathe
4	AdigoAditya(Padyam)	Satya Harichandra
6	Alatheilladha	Nala Damayanthi
7	Anuragadale	Vaalmiki
8	Baalondunandana	Jenugudu
9	BaaraaDhayathaaraa	Jagadekaveerana Kathe
10	Bhagavan	Vaalmiki
12	Bhayavyatake	Maduvemadinodu
13	BhuBhara	
14	Chaturambodhi	
15	Dashakantanadu	Chandrasena
16	Deva	Haribhakta
17	DevaDevaNarayana	Sri Krishnarjuna Yudha
18	DevaNinnaraajyadha	
19	DEVIPRAPANNARTI(PADYAM)_ AAADIPADI	
20	Dundumalle	
21	EanoEntho	Amarasilpi Jakkanachari
22	EEDEHA	Ohileswara
24	ElliHombelekelli	Saakumagalu
25	Hanumanaprana	Sree Ramanjaneya Yudha

26	HeChandrachuda	Satya Harichandra
27	Helidamathe	Saakumagalu
28	Jagamella	Maduvemadinodu
29	Jayajaya lokavana	Mahadeswara Puja Mahima
31	JayaJayaNataraja_Valmiki	Vaalmiki
32	Kayitan	
33	Kuladalli	Satya Harichandra
34	MaduveMaadiNoodu	Maduvemadinodu
36	Mahathma Kabir_Naguthiru chandaa_Ghantasala_Anusuua Devi	Mahatma Kabir
37	ManavuPrema	Sri Krishnarjuna Yudha
38	Mayaprapancheda	
39	Mellusiri	Veerakesari
40	Mugamuchi	Veerakesari
41	Nammoorachennayya	Muriyada Mane
42	Namobhutanadha_Kannada	Satya Harichandra
43	Nanadevadhanangalu(Padyam)_Kannada	Satya Harichandra
44	Nanatallu(Padyam)_Kannada	
45	Nanyake	Galigopura
46	Neeneyo	
47	Ninaguv	
48	Nutavu	
49	Nyayamidena	Satya Harichandra
50	ODivyaRamani	Jagadekaveerana Kathe
51	ONamaBarada	Veerakesari

52	Ondagibaluva	Jenugudu
53	PrajaraMaatannu	Veerakesari
54	RamaLakshmana	Veerakesari
55	Saagali	Mayabazar
56	SaaladheEePooje	Sri Krishnarjuna Yudha
57	Sakala	
58	Sakhitharave	Sri Krishnarjuna Yudha
59	Sathi Shakti_Devi prapannarthi_ Padyams_Ghantasala_TG Lingappa	Sathi Shakti
60	Satyavanu(Padyam)_Kannada	
61	Sivasankari	Jagadekaveerana Kathe
62	SriRamayana	
63	SriRamayana1	
64	Sundari	Mayabazar
65	Swabhimaanada	Veerakesari
66	Talikattida(Padyam)_Kannada	
67	TapavuPhalisidhee	Sri Krishnarjuna Yudha
68	Tulyanama	
69	Twamadidevata(Padyam)	Sri Krishna gaarudi
70	Vamsavanu(Padyam)_Kannada	Satya Harichandra
71	Vande(Slokam)	Satya Harichandra
72	Vichitravy	
73	Vidhivipareeta	Satya Harichandra
74	Vidhivipareeta1	Satya Harichandra
75	Yaarige	Galigopura
76	YaaroYaroo	Maduvemadinodu
77	Yarbartaro	Maduvemadinodu

78	Yavakaviya	Chandrahasa
79	Yellamangala	
80	Yelli	
81	Yenidi	Satya Harichandra
82	YenuduEevarase	

Annexure III
Malayalam songs

S. No	Name of the Malayalam song	Name of the movie
1	001_Karmaphalame	Aashadeepam
2	002_Logame	Aathmasakhi
3	003_Maata	Amma
4	004_PaduPadu	Naattiyatara
5	005_Kottakodu	Naattiyatara
6	006_Papamanithu Baale	Jeevitanouka
7	007_Snehame Lokam	Lokaneethi

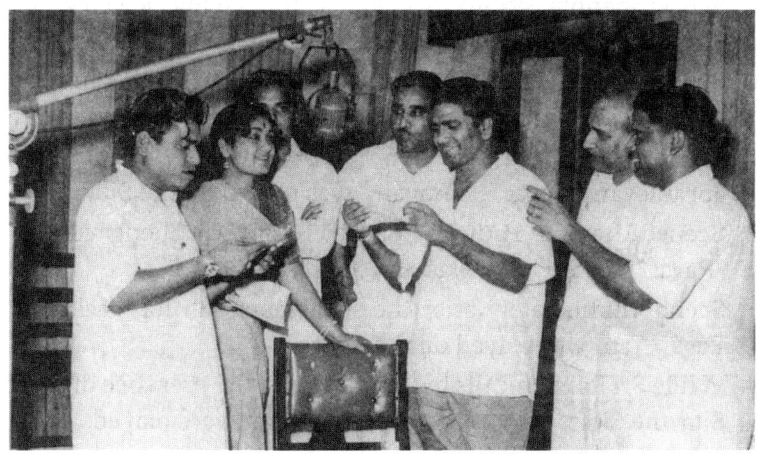

Annexure IV
The role of Pandit Janardan's Sitar in the movie "Lavakusa"

1. Scene: Sita and Rama stand before the statue of Surya Deva. Raga: In the background "Tillang" was played on the Sitar
2. Scene: After the padyam "Saptashwaratha Marudam." Raga: "Tillang" was played on the Sitar
3. Scene: During "Sitalankarana". Raga: "Yaman" was played on the Sitar
4. Scene: When Sita talks to her father King Janaka. Raga: "Dijaavanti & Bhageshwari" were played on the Sitar & Violin.
5. Scene: After decorating herself before going to the forest, Sita does "Paadabhivandana" to Rama. Raga: "Chakravaka" was played on the Sitar
6. Scene: While Valmiki walks in the forest, the birth of the twins is announced. Raga: "Desi" on the Sitar
7. Scene: When Valmiki wants Lava and Kusha to sing the Ramayana all over the world. Raga: "Malkauns" was played on the Sitar
8. Scene: After the song "Oorake Kanneru Nimpa----, " Lava and Kusha tell their mother that they would go to Ajodhya. Raga: "Abheri" was played on the Sitar
9. Scene: people go to Sri Rama for giving jewelry. Raga: "Saudamini" was played on the Sitar
10. Scene: People actually hand over the Jewelry to Sri Rama. Raga: "Keeravani" was played on the Sitar
11. Scene: After the Padyam "Sriraghavam Dasarathmajam-aprameyam" Raga: "Keeravani" was played on the Sitar
12. Scene: After the Padyam "Bangaru Rangaru Chengavulu ----- "Raga: "Kalyani" raga was played on the Sitar
13. Scene: Immediately after the scene above in the background. Raga: "Yan" was played on the Sitar
14. While Sri Rama recalls his memories in the presence of Swarna Sita, the Sitar, the Violin and the Clarinet were played.